Table of Contents

Chapter 1: Introduction – AI and IA 1

Chapter 2: The History and Development of AI and IA................................. 15

Chapter 3: The Impact of AI and IA on Society and the Workforce 26

Chapter 4: Understanding the Synergy between AI and IA 36

Chapter 5: The Ethics of AI and IA... 47

Chapter 6: AI and IA in Healthcare.. 57

Chapter 7: The Ethical and Regulatory Challenges in Integrating AI and IA in Healthcare Introduction 69

Chapter 8: The Future of AI and IA 80

Chapter 9: Conclusion 92

Augmenting Intelligence

The Synergy between Artificial Intelligence and Intelligence Augmentation

Raï

Dedication

THIS BOOK IS DEDICATED to all the hard-working men and women out there that will be affected positively and negatively as we enter into a new, ever-changing world, some would say a new era. I continue to hear this expression that goes, "You may not have it worry about losing your job to AI, but you should indeed worry about losing your job to a human being that works with AI." Personally, every time I hear this expression, it makes me wonder. It causes no panic in my heart because it has at least given me a choice. I intend to make the best choices to prepare for the future while I have the time.

Acknowledgment

I AM GRATEFUL TO BEGIN by expressing my sincere appreciation to my family and friends, who have provided unwavering support throughout my writing journey. Your encouragement, patience, and love have been indispensable in helping me see this project through to completion.

Furthermore, I would like to extend my heartfelt thanks to my editor, whose expertise and guidance have been invaluable in shaping this book into its final form. Your insightful comments and meticulous attention to detail have significantly strengthened this work.

I am also deeply thankful to the numerous experts and professionals who generously contributed their time and shared their knowledge with me. Your perspectives and insights have enriched this book and made it even more compelling.

Secondly, I would like to acknowledge and express my gratitude to all those who played a significant role in bringing this book to life. From the web page designer, application designer, book cover designer, and everyone else whom I may have inadvertently omitted, thank you so much.

Finally, I wish to express my appreciation to the readers of this book, whose interest and engagement continue to inspire me to explore new ideas and share them with the world. Your feedback and support are incredibly valuable and mean everything to me.

This book has been a long and rewarding journey, and I could not have achieved it without the help of so many wonderful people. Once again, thank you from the bottom of my heart.

About the Author

I'M AN ARMY VETERAN and SoCal resident looking to learn some new things. AI and IA have been one of my favorite subjects for the last year or so. In the late 1980s, my father used to say that one day, robots will take all of our jobs. I was about 10 years old and didn't really know what to think about it. Seems like my old man was on to something. Cant wait to see my wife and child flourish as we all learn these new tools together. Thank you all for purchasing my book. On to the future!

Chapter 1: Introduction – AI and IA

Overview of AI and IA

IN AN AGE WHERE TECHNOLOGY is progressing at an unprecedented pace, two paradigms have taken the forefront: Artificial Intelligence (AI) and Intelligence Augmentation (IA). Together, these paradigms stand as pillars supporting our relentless quest for technological advancement and societal transformation.

Definition and Key Differences

ARTIFICIAL INTELLIGENCE (AI), in the words of luminary scholars Russell, Norvig, and Davis, is akin to creating digital ambassadors that perceive the world, devise strategies, and make decisions to realize their objectives (Russell et al., 2010). These ambassadors, or AI systems, are crafted to echo human cognition, performing tasks that we consider distinctly human.

They comprehend our languages, discern patterns in chaos, unravel complex problems, and learn from their experiences, much like a child growing and adapting to the world around them.

AI's potential is not tied to human oversight; in fact, it can operate independently of us. It can be our reliable co-pilot in autonomous vehicles, ensuring safe travels, or it can act as our digital personal assistant, keeping our lives organized. AI's ability to automate tasks spreads across various fields, like an invisible web connecting and enhancing diverse aspects of human life.

On the other hand, *Intelligence Augmentation (IA)*, also known as cognitive augmentation or machine-augmented intelligence, aims not to replace human intelligence but to enhance it. According to Engelbart and Friedewald, IA is a field that "develops methods that can combine human and machine capabilities for better outcomes" (Engelbart & Friedewald, 1997). In other words, IA focuses on using technology as a tool to amplify human abilities, improving decision-making, problem-solving, and creative skills.

The fundamental difference between AI and IA lies in their primary goals. Where AI seeks to emulate and possibly surpass human intelligence, IA strives to complement and enhance it. While both paradigms share some commonalities, their differing objectives influence how society develops, implements, and perceives them.

Importance of AI and IA in Technology and Computer Science

AI AND IA HAVE BECOME indispensable in technology and computer science, drastically altering how we interact with digital platforms and, by extension, the world around us.

AI's importance is evident in its ubiquity and diverse applications. AI has infiltrated every aspect of our digital lives, from powering search engine algorithms that provide personalized search results, like Google's RankBrain (Sullivan, 2015), to enabling facial recognition systems in smartphones. It has also streamlined business processes, improved customer experiences, and has significant implications in areas such as healthcare, finance, and transportation (Makridakis, 2017).

IA, on the other hand, is equally critical. Engelbart's vision of "augmenting human intellect" has inspired the development of numerous technologies, including knowledge management systems, decision support systems, and advanced analytical tools that aid humans in processing complex data and making informed decisions (Engelbart & Friedewald, 1997). Moreover, IA plays a pivotal role in enabling us to tackle problems beyond our cognitive reach by extending our intellectual abilities (Licklider, 1960).

In computer science, both paradigms continue to inspire new algorithms, architectures, and systems. They have catalyzed research in fields such as machine learning, neural networks, human-computer interaction, and data mining, driving continuous innovation. As such, AI and IA represent two complementary paths in the pursuit of advanced intelligence. Both paradigms hold profound potential for technological advancement and societal transformation, forming the backbone of our ongoing digital revolution.

AI: Artificial Intelligence

IN OUR EXPLORATION of the interface between artificial intelligence and intelligence augmentation, it is fitting to delve deeper into each concept, starting with artificial intelligence. As one of the most transformative technologies of our time, understanding AI's nuances is crucial in appreciating its impact and potential.

Definition and Goals of AI

ARTIFICIAL INTELLIGENCE, or AI, forms a fascinating branch of the grand tree of computer science. Its essence lies in nurturing and shaping machines to perform tasks that have traditionally been in our human domain. From unraveling the complexities of human language, absorbing knowledge from experiences, identifying patterns in seeming randomness, to making informed decisions—these are the tasks AI breathes life into machines for (Russell et al., 2010).

Like teaching a child to navigate the world, the end goal of AI is to enable machines to function independently, capable of learning, adapting, and tackling complex problems, much like an autonomous explorer on an endless voyage of discovery.

AI's ambitions could be viewed as twofold, akin to a bird spreading its wings for flight. The first goal is to craft expert systems, entities that embody intelligent behavior with an inherent ability to learn, demonstrate their knowledge, explain their reasoning, and offer advice to users, much like an experienced mentor guiding a novice.

The second aspiration is to develop systems that grasp, learn, adapt, and ultimately mirror human intelligence within their digital confines (Nilsson, 1998). It's about building machines that don't just calculate and process but truly understand and evolve, much like humans in their endless journey of learning and growth.

Narrow AI (Weak AI) and General AI (Strong AI)

ARTIFICIAL INTELLIGENCE can be classified into two types: Narrow AI, also known as Weak AI, and General AI, or Strong AI.

Narrow AI is a type of AI that is designed to perform a specific task, such as voice recognition. This kind of AI operates under a limited set of constraints and is focused on a single, narrow task (Russell et al., 2010). An example would be Siri, Apple's virtual assistant, which can assist users in tasks like setting reminders or searching the internet but cannot perform tasks outside of its programmed domain.

On the other hand, *General AI*, often referred to as Strong AI, is an AI system with generalized human cognitive abilities, meaning it can understand, learn, adapt, and implement any intellectual task that a human being can (Searle, 1980). This type of AI is not currently in existence but remains a major goal of many AI research endeavors.

Examples of AI Applications

AI HAS FOUND ITS WAY into a myriad of applications, affecting numerous sectors of society. Here are a few notable examples:

Healthcare: AI is transforming healthcare, from predictive analytics to robot-assisted surgery. For instance, Google's DeepMind has developed an AI system capable of diagnosing eye diseases as accurately as human doctors (De Fauw et al., 2018).

Autonomous Vehicles: AI is the linchpin for self-driving cars. Tesla, for instance, employs AI for its Autopilot functionality, enabling autonomous navigation on the road (Schoettle & Sivak, 2015).

Financial Services: AI-powered systems help detect fraudulent transactions and automate investment decisions. Robo-advisors, such as Betterment and Wealthfront, use AI to manage and balance investment portfolios (Bai, 2011).

Voice Recognition: AI-powered voice assistants like Amazon's Alexa, Apple's Siri, and Google Assistant have become common in homes worldwide, revolutionizing how we interact with technology (Luger & Sellen, 2016).

Thus, AI is no longer a future concept but a present reality. As AI continues to evolve, so will its potential to revolutionize numerous sectors, alter our way of life, and challenge our understanding of what machines can do.

IA : Intelligence Augmentation

A DEEPER UNDERSTANDING of the latter is instrumental in exploring the meeting points between artificial intelligence and intelligence augmentation. Intelligence Augmentation (IA), although not as popular a term as AI, holds an equally impactful role in our technologically advancing society.

Definition and Objectives of IA

INTELLIGENCE AUGMENTATION, known in shorthand as IA, might best be considered a powerful partnership between humans and technology. Visionary thinker Douglas Engelbart first conceived the term in the 1960s, when he imagined a world where technology served as an extension of the human mind—a bit like a pair of spectacles for the intellect (Engelbart & Friedewald, 1997).

IA has a different calling, unlike its sibling AI, whose mission is to breathe human-like intelligence into machines. Its goal isn't to replicate our thought processes in silicon but to uplift them, like a trusted mentor guiding us to think more critically and creatively.

IA aims to turn us into better decision-makers by enhancing our natural intelligence with the precision and speed of the digital world. It's not about creating machines that think like us, but about using machines to help us think better.

The fundamental objective of IA is to create systems that "shall interact with human intellects to form a truly symbiotic system where human capabilities are used for formulating problems and making hypotheses, while machine capabilities are used for auxiliary computations and the simulation of complex models" (Licklider, 1960).

Simply put, IA aims to empower humans to solve complex problems by assisting them with the computational capabilities of machines.

Collaborative Approach of IA

THE ESSENCE OF IA LIES in its collaborative approach. By coupling human creativity and judgment with the computational power of machines, IA aims to elevate human cognition to a higher level. The collaboration here is not merely in the sense of tools helping humans but as integral partners improving human cognition, an approach encapsulated in the term *cognitive partnership* (Norman, 1993).

This collaboration manifests itself in many forms. For instance, when engineers design complex structures, IA tools can aid in the computation of the physical stresses the structure may encounter, thus enabling the engineer to focus on the design's aesthetic and functional aspects. In this sense, IA expands the capabilities of human intellect rather than replacing it, creating a symbiotic relationship between man and machine.

Tools and Technologies in IA

A WIDE RANGE OF TOOLS and technologies wear the badge of IA, almost like invisible superheroes aiding us in our daily lives. Common ones include digital personal assistants like Google Assistant, Siri, and Alexa. These helpful companions have become our digital memory extensions, reminding us of appointments, digging up information, and connecting us to others, akin to trusted secretaries in the virtual world.

More sophisticated IA applications step into the role of our expert advisors, specifically in fields like healthcare and finance. Imagine a weathered detective sifting through mountains of evidence to crack a case—decision support systems perform a similar function. They analyze vast amounts of data and distill it into valuable, actionable information.

An example of this is IBM's Watson for Oncology, which uses advanced analytics and machine learning to examine a patient's medical history in detail and suggest treatment options—almost like a virtual oncologist assisting the human medical team (Aggarwal & Madhukar, 2017).

Not just confined to the realm of information processing, IA also enhances our sensory experiences. Augmented Reality (AR) and Virtual Reality (VR) technologies have emerged as shining stars in the IA cosmos. They amplify our sensory perception and provide immersive experiences, reshaping how we interact with and understand our environment, much like a digital lens augmenting our view of the world (Milgram et al., 1995).

IA offers a unique yet complementary angle to AI. It's not just about recreating human intelligence; instead, it's about echoing it, amplifying it, and lighting up the inherent brilliance of human intellect. By encouraging a symbiotic relationship between humans and machines, IA crafts a pathway for technological advancements, mirroring the intricacies of human intelligence and enhancing it.

Understanding AI and IA

THE INTRICATE DANCE between Artificial Intelligence (AI) and Intelligence Augmentation (IA) propels the evolution of technology and the enrichment of human experience. At first glance, the terms may seem synonymous, but they embody unique approaches and philosophical underpinnings. To fully appreciate the synergy between them, it is essential to understand the differences and the distinct roles they play.

AI: Mimicking Human Cognitive Functions

AI AIMS TO SIMULATE human cognitive functions such as learning, problem-solving, and decision-making. It strives to make machines behave intelligently and independently, leveraging techniques like machine learning and natural language processing to achieve this aim.

AI's ultimate ambition is to create General AI or Strong AI—machines that possess the full range of human cognitive abilities, including understanding, learning, and even consciousness (Searle, 1980). In essence, AI is about making machines more human-like in their cognitive capacity.

IA: Enhancing Human Intelligence and Capabilities

IA, IN CONTRAST, DOES not aim to mimic human intelligence but to enhance it. Instead of creating autonomous machines, IA focuses on building tools that support and amplify human capabilities, fostering a symbiotic relationship between humans and machines. The core tenet of IA is the belief that machines and humans excel at different tasks.

While machines are superior in speed, scale, and precision, humans are unparalleled in their ability to think creatively, make strategic decisions, and understand complex contexts (Norman, 1993). IA tools are designed to extend the reach of the human mind, not to replicate it.

Differences between AI and IA

THE PRIMARY DIFFERENCE between AI and IA lies in their objectives and approaches. AI seeks to create machines that mimic human intelligence, function autonomously, and surpass humans in specific tasks. In contrast, IA aims to enhance and extend human cognition, focusing on collaborative, symbiotic relationships between humans and machines.

Another distinction between AI and IA emerges when considering their interactions with people. AI systems, especially those that leverage machine learning, can sometimes appear as enigmatic 'black boxes,' generating decisions that may not be readily understandable to us humans. It's akin to conversing with someone who speaks a language we can't understand—they may be intelligent, but we struggle to grasp their logic or insights.

Contrastingly, IA systems are designed like open books, prioritizing transparency and interpretability. They work hand-in-hand with humans, akin to a trusted colleague or advisor, helping us navigate through decisions and providing support based on clear, understandable reasoning.

In essence, while both AI and IA are integral components of the grand tapestry of cognitive technologies, they embody different philosophical and practical directions. AI excels in its pursuit of mimicking human intelligence, and IA shines in its endeavor to enhance our intellectual capabilities.

But the harmony between them holds the true magic—the key to architecting a future where humans and machines not just coexist but thrive together. Here, machines don't merely automate tasks; they amplify our innate human strengths, helping us solve intricate problems and steer through an increasingly complex world.

Importance of Combining AI and IA

AS WE JOURNEY DEEPER into the intricate world of Artificial Intelligence (AI) and Intelligence Augmentation (IA), the interplay between these two forces emerges like an intricate dance choreographed to perfection. The marriage of AI and IA has the potential to spawn systems that blend the best of both worlds, harmoniously intertwining AI's autonomy with the human-centric ethos of IA.

It's not just about building smarter machines but about kindling a partnership between silicon and neurons, each empowering the other toward a shared goal of discovery and innovation.

Complementary Relationship Between AI and IA

THE INTERSECTION OF AI and IA represents a sweet spot where the benefits of both paradigms are realized. AI, with its capacity to mimic and possibly surpass human intelligence in specific tasks, brings to the table the power of automation and machine learning. On the other hand, IA offers the advantage of enhancing human intellect by emphasizing collaboration and cognitive partnership between humans and machines (Norman, 1993).

This symbiosis leads to systems that can perform tasks independently, learn from their experiences (AI), and simultaneously augment human capabilities, promoting human-machine symbiosis (IA).

This complementary relationship opens new possibilities for innovative technological solutions that can address complex problems and enhance human potential.

Benefits of Combining AI and IA

THE INTEGRATION OF AI and IA leads to several benefits:

- **Efficiency and Effectiveness:** AI brings the ability to process vast amounts of data quickly and accurately, while IA provides context-sensitive interpretations and decisions. The combination results in systems that are both efficient and effective.

- **Learning and Adaptability:** AI's ability to learn from data and adapt over time complements IA's aim to enhance human learning, leading to a mutually beneficial learning environment.

- **User-centered Design:** IA's human-centric approach can ensure that AI technologies are designed with human needs and capabilities in mind, leading to more usable and effective systems.

Challenges in Integrating AI and IA

DESPITE THE POTENTIAL benefits, integrating AI and IA presents several challenges:

- **Interpretability and Transparency:** AI, especially deep learning models, can often act as black boxes, making decisions that are not easily interpretable by humans. This poses a challenge to IA's goal of enhancing human decision-making.

- **Data Privacy:** Both AI and IA rely heavily on data, raising concerns about privacy and security.

- **Ethical Considerations:** Questions about responsibility, control, and the potential for misuse of technology become even more complex when AI and IA are combined.

The fusion of AI and IA represents a promising path for the future of technology. The potential benefits are enormous, but realizing them requires careful navigation of the associated challenges. As we continue to explore this synergy, it is crucial to keep the focus on augmenting human potential and ensuring the responsible use of technology.

Conclusion

IN OUR EXPLORATION of Artificial Intelligence (AI) and Intelligence Augmentation (IA), we've seen two paradigms that, although distinct, intertwine in an intricate dance. They both hold the potential to change the way we live and work, revolutionize industries, and usher in new eras of technological innovation.

Significance of Finding the Right Balance Between AI and IA

THE RELATIONSHIP BETWEEN AI and IA is not one of competition but of symbiosis. Both paradigms bring unique strengths, and their integration can lead to systems that outperform what either could achieve alone. AI provides the power of autonomous decision-making and learning, while IA ensures these capabilities are harnessed to augment human potential, not replace it.

Finding the right balance between AI and IA is crucial for creating technologies that benefit society. Too much focus on AI could lead to efficient systems that lack transparency and usability. On the other hand, an overemphasis on IA could limit the scope of automation and the benefits that AI can offer.

Future Developments at the Intersection of AI and IA

THE SYNERGY BETWEEN AI and IA will continue to shape the future of technology. As AI systems become more capable, they will be increasingly used to augment human capabilities. For instance, we could see more advanced personal digital assistants that can understand and anticipate our needs or decision-support systems that can analyze complex data and offer actionable insights.

At the same time, IA principles will play a crucial role in guiding the development of these systems. Ensuring that AI technologies are human-centered, interpretable, and ethical will be key. IA can help ensure that as AI advances, it does so in a way that benefits and empowers humans.

AI and IA represent two sides of the same coin in our quest for advanced intelligence. By understanding and integrating these paradigms, we can create technologies that are powerful, efficient, and aligned with human needs and values.

References

BAI, S. (2011). ARTIFICIAL intelligence technologies in business and engineering. https://doi.org/10.1049/CP.2011.0486

De Fauw, J., Ledsam, J. R., Romera-Paredes, B., Nikolov, S., Tomasev, N., Blackwell, S., ... & Ronneberger, O. (2018). Clinically applicable deep learning for diagnosis and referral in retinal disease. Nature Medicine, 24(9), 1342-1350.

Engelbart, D. C., & Friedewald, M. (1997). *Augmenting human intellect: A conceptual framework*. Stanford Research Institute.

Aggarwal, M., & Madhukar, M. (2017). IBM's Watson analytics for health care: A miracle made true. In *Cloud Computing Systems and Applications in Healthcare* (pp. 117-134). IGI Global.

Licklider, J. C. R. (1960). Man-Computer Symbiosis. IRE Transactions on Human Factors in Electronics, HFE-1, 4-11.

Luger, E., & Sellen, A. (2016). Like having a really bad PA: The gulf between user expectation and experience of conversational agents. In Proceedings of the 2016 CHI Conference on Human Factors in Computing Systems (pp. 5286-5297).

Makridakis, S. (2017). The forthcoming Artificial Intelligence (AI) revolution: Its impact on society and firms. Futures, 90, 46-60.

Milgram, P., Takemura, H., Utsumi, A., & Kishino, F. (1995). Augmented reality: A class of displays on the reality-virtuality continuum. In Telemanipulator and Telepresence Technologies (Vol. 2351, pp. 282-292). International Society for Optics and Photonics.

Nilsson, N. J. (1998). Artificial intelligence: a new synthesis. Morgan Kaufmann.

Norman, D. (1993). Things that make us smart: Defending human attributes in the age of the machine. Addison-Wesley.

Russell, S. J., Davis, E., Norvig, P. (2009). Artificial Intelligence: A Modern Approach. United Kingdom: Prentice Hall.

Schoettle, B., & Sivak, M. (2015). A public opinion survey about autonomous and self-driving vehicles in the US, the UK, and Australia. The University of Michigan Transportation Research Institute.

Searle, J. R. (1980). Minds, brains, and programs. Behavioral and Brain Sciences, 3(3), 417-424.

Sullivan, D. (2015). FAQ: All About The New Google RankBrain Algorithm. Search Engine Land.

Chapter 2: The History and Development of AI and IA

The Dawn of a New Era: Early Concepts and Developments

ARTIFICIAL INTELLIGENCE (AI) and Intelligence Augmentation (IA) seeds were sown long before modern technology's advent. From ancient automata to modern computers, humanity's fascination with creating intelligent machines and enhancing human intellect has shaped centuries of technological innovation.

The Concept of Automated Machines in Ancient History

THE DREAM OF CREATING intelligent machines has ancient roots. One of the earliest recorded automata was the legendary 'automatic servant' of Hephaestus in the ancient Greek myths (Mayor, 2018). The idea was not confined to Greece, as mechanical figures found in ancient Egypt and China also testify to humanity's long-standing fascination with creating automated machines.

Ancient automata were simple by today's standards, typically relying on mechanical gears and levers. Still, they represented early steps toward developing machines that could carry out human-like tasks independently, a concept central to AI and IA.

Early Thought Experiments and Theoretical Foundations

THE EARLY THEORETICAL foundations for AI and IA were laid through thought experiments and philosophical investigations. René Descartes, a 17th-century philosopher, posited that animals were 'automata,' machines governed by physical laws (Descartes, 2008). This was an early hint at the idea that human-like Intelligence could be replicated in machines.

In the 19th century, Charles Babbage's Analytical Engine, although never fully built, represented a significant theoretical development (Swade, 2002). It was designed to use punch cards to conduct computations, hinting at the programmable machines that would later form the bedrock of modern computer science.

The Birth of Modern Computer Science

THE BIRTH OF MODERN computer science brought the concepts of AI and IA closer to reality. Alan Turing, widely recognized as the father of theoretical computer science, proposed the idea of a 'universal machine' capable of simulating any computable sequence (Turing, 1936). Turing's work laid the groundwork for the modern programmable computer.

Moreover, his famous *Turing Test* offered a practical definition of machine intelligence: a machine could be considered intelligent if it could convince a human observer that it, too, was human (Turing, 2009). This idea marked a significant step in the journey toward AI.

The birth of modern computer science also saw the development of the first digital computers. These machines, although primitive by today's standards, provided the technological infrastructure necessary to explore AI and IA further.

The Emergence of Artificial Intelligence

AS THE FOUNDATIONS of computer science were laid and computers began to evolve from room-sized behemoths to more compact and powerful machines, the path was cleared for the birth of a revolutionary field: Artificial Intelligence (AI).

Early AI Research and Key Contributors

AS A DISTINCT FIELD, artificial Intelligence took shape in the mid-20th century. John McCarthy coined the term Artificial Intelligence at the Dartmouth Conference in 1956, often considering the birth of AI as a separate field (McCarthy et al., 2006). The conference brought together pioneers like Marvin Minsky, Allen Newell, and Herbert A. Simon, whose collective contributions would shape AI's trajectory for years to come.

AI's early years were marked by optimism. Researchers aimed to create machines capable of performing any intellectual task that a human being can do. These early endeavors focused on problem-solving, learning, and natural language understanding, paving the way for future advancements (Crevier, 1993).

Milestones in AI Development: From ELIZA to AlphaGo

SEVERAL SIGNIFICANT milestones mark AI's evolution. ELIZA, developed by Joseph Weizenbaum at MIT in the mid-1960s, was one of the first programs to demonstrate the possibility of a machine conducting a conversation in natural language (Weizenbaum, 1965).

Fast forward to the 1990s, when IBM's Deep Blue defeated the world chess champion, Garry Kasparov, demonstrating AI's capability to excel in complex strategic games (Campbell et al., 2002).

More recently, Google's AlphaGo program, designed to play the board game Go, defeated the world champion Go player in 2016 (Silver et al., 2016). Go is known for its complexity and requires strategic thinking and intuition, which made this victory a significant leap forward for AI.

Evolution of AI: Machine Learning and Deep Learning

IN THE NURTURING WOMB of AI, distinct fields like Machine Learning (ML) and Deep Learning (DL) have taken form and flourished. Much like a master potter shaping clay, ML focuses on sculpting algorithms that learn from data, refining their performance over time and becoming increasingly adept with each experience. DL, a sub-field of ML, takes its inspiration from the intricate neural networks that define our brains. It has pushed the boundaries of AI, driving notable advancements in areas like image and speech recognition, akin to gifting machines with a crude sense of sight and sound (LeCun et al., 2015).

The journey of AI, from its humble beginnings to its present-day triumphs, is more than just a tale of machines and codes. It's a testament to the triumph of human imagination and creativity. As we've coached machines to echo aspects of human Intelligence, we've not only revolutionized our technological landscape but also embarked on a journey of introspection, prompting us to better understand the contours and capabilities of our intellect.

The Rise of Intelligence Augmentation

WHILE AI HAS OFTEN stolen the spotlight, another compelling, parallel narrative has unfolded in the shadow of our drive to make machines think: the story of Intelligence Augmentation (IA). IA does not seek to create a machine version of human Intelligence but to amplify our inherent human intellectual capacities. Let's delve into the origins, the key milestones, and the evolution of this incredible field.

Douglas Engelbart and the Concept of IA

THE TERM INTELLIGENCE Augmentation can be traced back to a visionary named Douglas Engelbart. In the 1960s, Engelbart proposed the idea of using computers not just for automation but to "augment human intellect" to fundamentally enhance our ability to solve complex problems (Engelbart & Friedewald, 1997). Unlike AI's mission to emulate human cognition, Engelbart saw technology as a partner to human intellect, a tool to help us think better, make decisions more effectively, and expand our cognitive horizons.

Notable Advancements and Applications in IA

THROUGHOUT THE ENSUING decades, Engelbart's pioneering vision inspired a plethora of advancements. The development of personal computing interfaces in the 1970s and 1980s, for instance, allowed more people to leverage the power of computers for individual tasks, embodying the principles of IA (Shneiderman, 2003).

Decision support systems were developed in the medical field to help doctors diagnose diseases and plan treatments. One such system, IBM's Watson for Oncology, uses advanced analytics to recommend personalized treatment plans, effectively augmenting the doctor's decision-making process (Kohli & Tan, 2016).

In our everyday lives, digital personal assistants like Siri, Alexa, and Google Assistant help us manage our tasks and access information quickly, effectively enhancing our ability to manage and recall information (Luger & Sellen, 2016).

IA's Evolution in the Digital Age

AS WE CRUISE THE CURRENTS of the digital age, IA unfurls its sails, navigating broader seas of technological possibility. Today, IA wraps its arms around an impressive array of technologies. It welcomes into its fold augmented reality (AR) and virtual reality (VR) systems, which paint richer hues onto our perception of the world, and sophisticated analytics tools that amplify our ability to untangle and interpret complex webs of data (Milgram et al., 1995).

Furthermore, the principles of IA are not content with being confined to their domain. They are nudging their way into the architectural blueprints of AI, advocating for a human-centered design ethos. The clamor is growing louder for AI systems that don't just replace human capacities but augment our decision-making abilities and enrich our skillset.

As we chart our course through the digital age, the guiding star of IA continues to illuminate our journey. Its philosophy shapes our approach to technology, reminding us that our tools are not our masters but our aides.

It ensures that technology amplifies our inherent human strengths and capabilities rather than casting them into its shadow. It nudges us toward a future where humans and machines collaborate, each augmenting the other, in a symbiotic dance of intellect and innovation.

Synergies and Interactions: AI and IA Together

WHILE AI AND IA EACH possess distinctive qualities and objectives, their combined power paints a fascinating picture. Working in synergy, this dynamic duo brings the best of both worlds—the autonomy of AI dancing in harmony with the human-centered focus of IA.

Early Interactions and Synergies Between AI and IA

SINCE THE EARLY DAYS of computer science, the paths of AI and IA have been closely intertwined. While AI researchers were dreaming of creating machines that could think like humans, pioneers like Engelbart explored how these machines could augment human intellect (Engelbart & Friedewald, 1997). Both sought to harness the power of computers to enhance human capabilities, albeit in different ways.

The development of expert systems in the 1970s and 1980s exemplifies this synergy. These AI-based systems were designed to emulate the decision-making ability of a human expert, thus augmenting human decision-making in complex areas such as medical diagnosis and financial planning (Shortliffe & Buchanan, 1975).

Notable Combined Applications of AI and IA

OVER TIME, THE INTERPLAY between AI and IA has given rise to numerous innovative applications. For instance, in healthcare, AI algorithms analyze vast amounts of medical data, providing insights that can help doctors make more informed decisions (Topol, 2019). Here, the machine's 'intelligence' (AI) is used to augment the physician's expertise (IA).

Similarly, in education, AI-powered adaptive learning systems modify content in real-time based on a student's performance, effectively personalizing learning and augmenting the teacher's ability to cater to individual student needs (Pane et al., 2014).

Current Trends and Developments in Combining AI and IA

THE MEETING POINT OF AI and IA is fertile ground from which current technological trends continue to sprout. One such growth is the emergence of Explainable AI (XAI)—AI systems that don't merely make decisions but narrate their thought process in a language we understand (Gunning, 2019).

This shift is akin to a once aloof librarian guiding us to the books we need and explaining why those books are the best fit for our inquiries. By doing so, XAI doesn't just enable us to use AI but also allows us to trust it, further entwining our human abilities with AI's capabilities.

Moreover, as AI steadily weaves itself into the tapestry of our lives, there's a growing consensus about the significance of keeping these technologies human-centric. With its human-empowering principles, IA steps into the role of a mentor, ensuring that AI doesn't lose sight of its ultimate purpose—to augment human Intelligence and abilities, not supersede them.

These principles remind us that technology, in its most beautiful form, is not a usurper but an ally, a tool that illuminates and amplifies the incredible facets of our humanity.

In sum, the interplay between AI and IA represents an exciting frontier in our journey toward creating intelligent machines. By combining the power of AI with the principles of IA, we can create systems that are not only intelligent but also designed to enhance our inherent human capacities.

Conclusion: Reflection on the Journey and Future Prospects

AS WE TRACE THE INTRICATE tapestry of AI and IA's history, it's clear that these fields are not just about machines and algorithms. They represent a profound human journey, a testament to our insatiable curiosity, creativity, and ambition.

Major Breakthroughs and Turning Points

FROM ANCIENT AUTOMATA to modern algorithms, the journey of AI and IA has been marked by several significant breakthroughs. The invention of programmable digital computers laid the technological groundwork for these fields. Key milestones such as Turing's universal machine, Engelbart's vision of augmented intellect, the development of expert systems, and the rise of machine learning and deep learning have turned what was once science fiction into reality.

The major turning point in AI came when researchers started developing algorithms that could learn from data, moving away from rule-based systems. This shift paved the way for contemporary AI technologies like deep learning (LeCun et al., 2015).

In the IA realm, the rise of personal computing was a significant inflection point. For the first time, technology that could augment human intellect became accessible to the masses (Shneiderman, 2003).

Current State of AI and IA Development

TODAY, AI AND IA STAND as influential fields transforming various aspects of society, from healthcare and education to entertainment and communication. We've taught machines to diagnose diseases, drive cars, beat humans at complex board games, and even generate art. Meanwhile, we're also seeing how technology can enhance our abilities, helping us make better decisions, learn more effectively, and interact with the world in new and exciting ways.

Looking Forward: The Future of AI and IA

LOOKING FORWARD, THE confluence of AI and IA holds enormous promise. The development of AI systems that respect human autonomy, incorporate human feedback, and explain their decisions transparently aligns with the principles of IA and represents a promising trend in AI (Gunning, 2019).

As we stand on the brink of tomorrow, the future likely holds an intensified harmony between AI and IA, crafting technologies that marry the strengths of both worlds. We can envision autonomous, intelligent machines that aren't there to replace us but to join hands with us. These machines will amplify our abilities and serve as steadfast companions, helping us traverse an increasingly intricate world.

As we step forward into this thrilling future, it's vital to remember the common thread that weaves AI and IA together—the aspiration to uplift human life. This shared goal seeks to fan the flames of our capabilities, aiming to foster a future where humans and machines are not adversaries but allies.

It dreams of a harmonious duet where our human intellect dances with machine intelligence, choreographing a world where we lean on each other's strengths to craft a shared symphony of progress.

References

CAMPBELL, M., HOANE Jr, A. J., & Hsu, F. H. (2002). Deep blue. *Artificial Intelligence, 134*(1-2), 57-83.

Crevier, D. (1993). AI: The Tumultuous History of the Search for Artificial Intelligence. Basic Books.

Descartes, R. (2008). Discourse on the Method. United States: Cosimo, Incorporated.

Engelbart, D. C., & Friedewald, M. (1997). *Augmenting human intellect: A conceptual framework*. Stanford Research Institute.

Gunning, D. (2019). Explainable Artificial Intelligence (XAI). Defense Advanced Research Projects Agency (DARPA), nd Web, 2(2).

Kohli, M., & Tan, S. S. (2016). Electronic health records: how can IS researchers contribute to transforming healthcare? MIS Quarterly, 40(3), 553-573.

LeCun, Y., Bengio, Y., & Hinton, G. (2015). Deep learning. Nature, 521(7553), 436-444.

Luger, E., & Sellen, A. (2016). "Like Having a Really Bad PA": The Gulf between User Expectation and Experience of Conversational Agents. Proceedings of the 2016 CHI Conference on Human Factors in Computing Systems, 5286-5297.

Mayor, A. (2018). Gods and Robots: Myths, Machines, and Ancient Dreams of Technology. Princeton University Press.

McCarthy, J., Minsky, M. L., Rochester, N., & Shannon, C. E. (2006). A proposal for the dartmouth summer research project on artificial Intelligence, august 31, 1955. *AI magazine, 27*(4), 12-12.

Milgram, P., Takemura, H., Utsumi, A., & Kishino, F. (1995, December). Augmented reality: A class of displays on the reality-virtuality continuum. In *Telemanipulator and telepresence technologies* (Vol. 2351, pp. 282-292). Spie.

Pane, J. F., Steiner, E. D., Baird, M. D., & Hamilton, L. S. (2015). Continued Progress: Promised Findings from a RAND Study of Carnegie Learning's Cognitive Tutor Algebra I in High-Need Schools. RAND Corporation.

Shneiderman, B. (2003). Leonardo's Laptop: Human Needs and the New Computing Technologies. MIT Press.

Shortliffe, E. H., & Buchanan, B. G. (1975). A model of inexact reasoning in medicine. Mathematical Biosciences, 23(3-4), 351-379.

Silver, D., Huang, A., Maddison, C. J., Guez, A., Sifre, L., Van Den Driessche, G., ... & Hassabis, D. (2016). Mastering the game of Go with deep neural networks and tree search. *nature*, 529(7587), 484-489.

Swade, D., Babbage, C. (2002). The Difference Engine: Charles Babbage and the Quest to Build the First Computer. United States: Penguin Books.

Topol, E. (2019). Deep Medicine: How Artificial Intelligence Can Make Healthcare Human Again. Basic Books.

Turing, A. M. (2009). *Computing machinery and intelligence* (pp. 23-65). Springer Netherlands.

Turing, A. M. (1936). On Computable Numbers: With an Application to the Entscheidungsproblem. United Kingdom: Mathematical Society.

Weizenbaum, J. (1965). Eliza: a Computer Program for the Study of Natural Language Communication Between Man and Machine. United States: MIT.

Chapter 3: The Impact of AI and IA on Society and the Workforce

Understanding the Societal Impact of AI and IA

OUR LIVES ARE WOVEN with invisible threads of AI and IA that influence and shape our daily experiences. From simple tasks to complex decisions, these technologies have etched an indelible impact on our society. However, along with their gifts come some challenges, particularly in the spheres of privacy, security, and ethics.

How AI and IA Influence Daily Life

WE ENGAGE IN A SILENT dialogue with AI and IA daily, often without realizing it. From morning alarms that adapt to our sleep patterns to social media feeds tailored to our interests and digital assistants that simplify tasks, our lives are subtly intertwined with these technologies. They aid us in navigating traffic, assist us in choosing what movie to watch, or even suggest the quickest checkout line at the grocery store (Russell, Davis, & Norvig, 2009).

On the other hand, IA tools such as augmented reality applications augment our daily experiences. They enhance our ability to interact with the world, enabling us to visualize furniture in our living room before purchasing it or overlay historical facts on landmarks as we tour a city (Milgram et al., 1995).

Impact on Privacy and Security

YET, THESE TECHNOLOGICAL marvels also pose challenges. As we entrust more of our personal information to AI systems, privacy and security concerns loom. AI algorithms that suggest personalized ads or predict our behavior often do so by analyzing vast amounts of personal data, leading to concerns about data misuse and breaches (Brundage et al., 2018).

Moreover, AI and IA technologies are becoming attractive targets for cyberattacks, raising concerns about the security of these systems. For example, if compromised, intelligent systems in autonomous vehicles or healthcare applications could lead to serious consequences (Taddeo et al., 2021).

Ethical Implications and Considerations

BEYOND PRIVACY AND security, AI and IA raise complex ethical questions. AI decision-making, for example, can unintentionally reinforce societal biases in the data used to train these systems. Such biases can lead to unfair outcomes in critical areas like hiring, lending, or law enforcement (Buolamwini & Gebru, 2018).

In the realm of IA, questions about human agency and responsibility arise. If an IA system aids in decision-making, who is responsible for the outcome of that decision?

As we weave AI and IA more deeply into our societal fabric, addressing these challenges head-on is crucial. This includes creating robust regulatory frameworks, fostering transparency and accountability in AI and IA systems, and promoting an ongoing dialogue about ethical considerations.

The Role of AI and IA in Different Industries

THE TENDRILS OF AI and IA stretch into various industries, transforming how we heal, learn, work, and play. Their impact is felt in the healthcare, medicine, education, finance, business, entertainment, and media industries. Each sector offers a unique canvas for the artistry of AI and IA, painting a future where innovation, efficiency, and personalization reign.

Healthcare and Medicine

IN THE REALM OF HEALTHCARE and medicine, AI and IA are revolutionizing patient care and research. AI algorithms help diagnose diseases, analyze medical images, and even predict patient outcomes, offering new avenues for precision medicine (Topol, 2019). IA, on the other hand, empowers healthcare professionals with enhanced decision-making capabilities. Tools like IBM's Watson for Oncology provide physicians with evidence-based treatment options, effectively augmenting their medical expertise (Aggarwal & Madhuykar, 2017).

Education

EDUCATION IS ANOTHER area significantly influenced by AI and IA. AI-powered adaptive learning systems offer personalized learning experiences, adjusting content to suit each student's unique learning pace and style (Pane et al., 2015). IA tools, such as AR and VR, enrich learning experiences, enabling students to explore historical events or scientific concepts in immersive, interactive ways (Merchant et al., 2014).

Finance and Business

AI AND IA HAVE RESHAPED the landscape of finance and business. AI algorithms assist in predicting market trends, detecting fraud, and personalizing customer experiences, driving efficiency and innovation. IA tools support decision-making, helping professionals navigate complex financial data and make informed business decisions.

Entertainment and Media

IN THE WORLD OF ENTERTAINMENT and media, AI and IA have dramatically altered content creation and consumption. AI is used in everything from movie recommendations to generating virtual characters. IA, with technologies like AR and VR, has redefined immersive entertainment, enabling us to step into virtual worlds or overlay digital information onto our physical environment.

The Influence of AI and IA on the Workforce

AI AND IA ARE RESHAPING the contours of the workforce, much like tides subtly yet relentlessly transforming a coastline. They create and displace jobs, alter the skill sets demanded, and redefine traditional work boundaries. The following sections delve into the changes these digital waves bring and how they ripple through our working lives.

Impact on Job Displacement and Creation

THE ADVENT OF AI AND IA has been both a boon and a bane for the workforce. On the one hand, these technologies automate routine tasks, leading to job displacement, particularly in manufacturing and administrative roles (Bessen, 2018). On the other hand, they create new jobs that require managing, developing, and interacting with AI and IA systems. A study by the World Economic Forum estimates that while 75 million jobs may be displaced by AI, 133 million new jobs could be created (World Economic Forum, 2018).

Changing Skill Requirements and Job Roles

AI AND IA ARE NOT JUST reshaping the job market but also altering the skills required and the very nature of work itself. As machines take over routine tasks, there's a growing demand for skills that machines can't replicate, such as complex problem-solving, creativity, and emotional intelligence (Bessen, 2018).

Furthermore, AI and IA are transforming traditional job roles, integrating into areas like healthcare, education, and finance, where professionals now work alongside these systems, leveraging their capabilities to enhance productivity and decision-making.

The Rise of Remote Work and Digital Nomadism

AI AND IA ALSO HAVE untethered work from physical locations, contributing to the rise of remote work and digital nomadism. Tools that support virtual collaboration and automated administrative tasks make it possible for people to work from anywhere, redefining traditional work arrangements and creating more flexible, inclusive opportunities (Kaplan & Haenlein, 2020).

The influence of AI and IA on the workforce is profound and multifaceted. As we adapt to this shifting landscape, we must also consider how we can ensure fair transitions and mitigate the adverse impacts.

AI, IA, and the Global Economy

THE FINGERPRINTS OF AI and IA are increasingly visible on the global economy's pulse. They contribute to economic growth, shape the patterns of wealth distribution, and impact the global competitive landscape. As we navigate this AI- and IA-induced economic transformation, we need to examine the remarkable benefits and potential challenges they bring.

Economic Benefits and Growth

AI AND IA CAN POTENTIALLY be major growth drivers for the global economy. Their ability to automate routine tasks, optimize operations, and uncover insights from vast amounts of data can significantly increase productivity. McKinsey Global Institute estimates that AI could add around $13 trillion to the global economy by 2030, boosting global GDP by about 1.2% yearly (Bughin et al., 2018).

Challenges to Economic Inequality

HOWEVER, THE ECONOMIC benefits of AI and IA are not spread evenly. These technologies could exacerbate economic inequality as industries heavily reliant on routine tasks face significant disruption, and the benefits accrue disproportionately to AI and IA innovators and investors (Bessen, 2018). Moreover, countries at the forefront of AI and IA development stand to gain the most, potentially widening the economic gap between nations. Policymakers worldwide must therefore work to ensure the benefits of AI and IA are broadly shared, both within and between nations.

Global Competitiveness and Geopolitics

AI AND IA ARE RESHAPING the global competitive landscape and are increasingly intertwined with geopolitics. Countries investing heavily in these technologies, like the United States and China, are poised to lead the next wave of economic growth (Lee, 2018). These technological advances also have significant geopolitical implications, influencing national security, surveillance, and the balance of power. The nations that master these technologies will likely substantially influence the future world order.

As AI and IA continue to weave themselves into the global economic fabric, we must approach the ensuing transformation with an eye for harnessing their potential, mitigating challenges, and ensuring the benefits reach all corners of our global community.

The Future: Building a Society with AI and IA

AS WE STAND AT THE crossroads of the present, with an eye toward the future, we recognize the role of AI and IA as architects of tomorrow's society. They promise a world replete with innovation and convenience but also one that demands new rules and considerations.

Anticipating Future Societal Changes

THE FUTURE PAINTED by AI and IA is akin to an impressionist masterpiece—each stroke representing a change in how we live, work, and interact. We can anticipate homes that adjust to our needs, education that adapts to each learner, and healthcare personalized to our genetic makeup (Russell, Davis, & Norvig, 2009). However, alongside these advancements come challenges—job displacement, privacy concerns, and ethical dilemmas—that society must be prepared to address.

The Role of Policy and Regulation

THE SOCIETAL TRANSFORMATION induced by AI and IA calls for comprehensive policy and regulatory frameworks. Policymakers are critical in managing this digital revolution, ensuring benefits are widely spread and mitigating adverse effects. They must address data privacy questions, the ethical use of AI and IA, job displacement, and the digital divide (Taddeo et al., 2021). Crafting these regulations is a delicate act of balance—ensuring safety and fairness without stifling innovation.

Ensuring an Inclusive, Equitable AI- and IA-Driven Future

AS WE STEP INTO THE AI- and IA-augmented future, we need to ensure it's a world where everyone benefits. This involves creating inclusive technologies, considering diverse user needs, promoting equitable access to AI and IA benefits, and equipping people with the skills needed for the future workforce (World Economic Forum, 2018).

The dawn of an AI- and IA-driven society holds great promise, but the path to realizing this future is not without hurdles. It requires a concerted effort from technologists, policymakers, and society as a whole to guide the transformation toward a future that reflects our shared values and aspirations.

Conclusion: Reflecting on the Impact and Looking Ahead

AS WE STEP BACK AND survey the landscape transformed by AI and IA, we recognize that we stand on the brink of a future that was once confined to the pages of science fiction. These technologies have been woven into our daily lives, fueling changes that ripple through our society, industries, workforce, and the global economy.

They paint a future rich with promise. We see glimpses of a world where healthcare is tailored to each individual, education adapts to each learner, and where the daunting barriers of language and geography crumble before our shared desire for connection.

Yet, with these promising horizons come challenges that cast long shadows. Issues of privacy, security, job displacement, and economic disparity demand our attention. The path we navigate into this future will not always be smooth, and our decisions will have profound implications for future generations.

In the face of these challenges, we are not powerless. We possess the tools to shape this future into a world that reflects our shared values and aspirations. The keys lie in proactive regulation, inclusive design, equitable access, and education that empowers everyone to thrive in an AI- and IA-augmented world.

In the chapters that follow, we will delve deeper into these aspects. We will explore strategies to ensure an inclusive and equitable future, examine the role of education and upskilling, and highlight the importance of an ethical framework for AI and IA.

As we venture into this future, we are reminded of the words of Alan Kay: "The best way to predict the future is to invent it." It is up to us to shape the role of AI and IA in our lives, crafting a world that mirrors our intellect and humanity.

References

AGGARWAL, M., & MADHUKAR, M. (2017). IBM's Watson analytics for health care: A miracle made true. In *Cloud Computing Systems and Applications in Healthcare* (pp. 117-134). IGI Global.

Bessen, J. (2018). Artificial intelligence and jobs: The role of demand. In *The economics of artificial intelligence: an agenda* (pp. 291-307). University of Chicago Press.

Brundage, M., Avin, S., Clark, J., Toner, H., Eckersley, P., Garfinkel, B., ... & Amodei, D. (2018). The malicious use of artificial intelligence: Forecasting, prevention, and mitigation. *arXiv preprint arXiv:1802.07228*.

Bughin, J., Seong, J., Manyika, J., Chui, M., & Joshi, R. (2018). Notes from the AI frontier: Modeling the impact of AI on the world economy. *McKinsey Global Institute, 4*.

Buolamwini, J., & Gebru, T. (2018). Gender Shades: Intersectional Accuracy Disparities in Commercial Gender Classification. Proceedings of the 1st Conference on Fairness, Accountability and Transparency, in PMLR 81:77-91.

Kaplan, A., & Haenlein, M. (2020). Rulers of the world, unite! The challenges and opportunities of artificial intelligence. Business Horizons, 63(1), 37-50.

Lee, K. F. (2018). AI Superpowers: China, Silicon Valley, and the New World Order. Houghton Mifflin Harcourt.

Merchant, Z., Goetz, E. T., Cifuentes, L., Keeney-Kennicutt, W., & Davis, T. J. (2014). Effectiveness of virtual reality-based instruction on students' learning outcomes in K-12 and higher education: A meta-analysis. Computers & Education, 70, 29-40.

Milgram, P., Takemura, H., Utsumi, A., & Kishino, F. (1995, December). Augmented reality: A class of displays on the reality-virtuality continuum. In *Telemanipulator and telepresence technologies* (Vol. 2351, pp. 282-292). Spie.

Pane, J. F., Steiner, E. D., Baird, M. D., & Hamilton, L. S. (2015). Continued Progress: Promised Findings from a RAND Study of Carnegie Learning's Cognitive Tutor Algebra I in High-Need Schools. RAND Corporation.

Russell, S. J., Davis, E., Norvig, P. (2009). Artificial Intelligence: A Modern Approach. United Kingdom: Prentice Hall.

Taddeo, M., McNeish, D., Blanchard, A., & Edgar, E. (2021). Ethical principles for artificial intelligence in national defence. *Philosophy & Technology, 34,* 1707-1729.

Topol, E. (2019). Deep Medicine: How Artificial Intelligence Can Make Healthcare Human Again. Basic Books.

World Economic Forum. (2018). The Future of Jobs Report 2018. World Economic Forum, Geneva, Switzerland.

Chapter 4: Understanding the Synergy between AI and IA

Introduction: The Intersection of AI and IA

AS WE VENTURE DEEPER into the era of digital revolution, we encounter two allies on this journey—Artificial Intelligence (AI) and Intelligence Augmentation (IA). Separately, they transform facets of our lives; together, they have the potential to redefine our world. Their intersection, an intertwining dance of technology, offers a compelling exploration into the power of synergy and integration.

The Power of Combining AI and IA

UNITING AI AND IA OPENS up a realm of possibilities that eclipse what each could accomplish in solitude. With its capacity to process colossal data and make complex decisions, AI brings forth efficiency and scale. However, IA enriches this with a human-centered approach, striving to enhance human capabilities and decision-making (Engelbart & Friedewald, 1997).

Their combination offers a holistic view of intelligent systems, marrying the strengths of human cognition—creativity, critical thinking, emotional understanding—with machines' unerring precision and tireless productivity. In this blend lies the potential to create systems that mimic or augment human intellect and elevate it to unparalleled levels.

Key Principles for Integrating AI and IA

WHILE PROMISING, AI and IA integration demands a thoughtful approach. It requires a commitment to certain key principles:

1. User-Centric Design: The primary aim of AI and IA should be to create user value. AI systems should be designed to be intuitive and adaptable, and IA tools should seamlessly augment human tasks (Norman, 2013).

2. Transparency: Users should understand how AI systems make decisions, particularly when those systems augment human decision-making. Transparency fosters trust, a crucial ingredient for widespread adoption (Ribeiro et al., 2016).

3. Interoperability: AI and IA systems should be able to communicate and work together efficiently. A system designed for IA should be able to leverage AI capabilities and vice versa (Norvig, Davis, & Russell, 2009).

4. Ethics: The combination of AI and IA should respect user privacy, ensure fairness, and prevent harm. Ethical guidelines should inform the design and implementation of these systems (Floridi & Cowls, 2022).

In embracing these principles, we pave the way for a future where AI and IA work in unison, bringing out the best in both human and machine capabilities.

AI and IA: Complementing Each Other

LIKE TWO PIECES OF a puzzle, AI and IA fit together to form a complete picture of cognitive technology's potential. They draw from each other's strengths and compensate for each other's weaknesses. They complement each other in remarkable ways—AI lending its computational prowess to IA's pursuit of enhanced human cognition, and IA instilling a human touch in AI's autonomous operations.

AI's Role in IA: Enhancing Cognitive Capacities

AI'S PART IN THIS COGNITIVE symphony is providing the powerful computational abilities to augment human intelligence. Its ability to process vast quantities of data and discern patterns provides a potent tool to extend our cognitive capabilities (LeCun, Bengio & Hinton, 2015).

AI technologies, such as machine learning algorithms, can aid in making sense of complex data, offering insights that can augment our decision-making process. Natural language processing (NLP) can enhance our ability to interact with digital devices using human language, blurring the boundaries between human and machine communication. And AI's potential for autonomous operation can take over routine tasks, freeing humans to engage in more creative, high-order cognitive tasks.

IA's Role in AI: Human-Centered AI Systems

ON THE OTHER SIDE OF the coin, IA contributes a human-centered approach to AI systems. It underscores the principle that technology should serve as a natural extension of human capabilities, emphasizing user-friendliness and empathy in design (Norman, 2013).

IA plays a pivotal role in ensuring that AI technologies align with human goals and values. It emphasizes the need for AI systems to be transparent and interpretable, ensuring users understand and trust the decisions made by AI. Furthermore, IA pushes for AI to be inclusive, ensuring it caters to diverse user needs and fostering an environment where technology amplifies human potential.

In essence, the roles of AI and IA in relation to each other underline the yin and yang of cognitive technologies. Their symbiotic relationship forms the cornerstone of building systems that can truly augment human intellect and capabilities while respecting and upholding our inherent human values.

Case Studies: Successful Integration of AI and IA

IN THIS SECTION, WE traverse across industries, exploring real-life applications where the synergy of AI and IA has begun to bear fruit. We'll venture through the healthcare, education, and business sectors, identifying how integrating AI and IA in these fields has unlocked new possibilities and brought about marked improvements in service delivery, personalization, and efficiency.

Healthcare: Improved Diagnosis and Patient Care

THE HEALTHCARE SECTOR stands as a testament to the power of AI and IA collaboration. Here, AI's ability to analyze large volumes of data, combined with IA's goal to augment human decision-making, results in improved diagnosis and patient care. For instance, IBM's Watson for Health uses AI to analyze a patient's medical history, current symptoms, and the latest medical research, providing healthcare professionals with actionable insights to augment their decision-making process (Kohli & Tan, 2016).

Such AI-powered IA tools are revolutionizing healthcare, providing personalized patient care, improving diagnosis accuracy, and helping healthcare professionals devise optimal treatment plans.

Education: Personalized Learning Experiences

IN THE FIELD OF EDUCATION, the AI-IA combination enables personalized learning experiences. Adaptive learning platforms like DreamBox Learning use AI algorithms to analyze a student's performance, adapting the content in real-time to provide personalized learning pathways (Dilmurod & Fazliddin, 2021).

By augmenting a teacher's capacity to cater to individual student needs, these platforms exemplify the successful fusion of AI and IA in education, enhancing teaching efficacy and facilitating personalized learning experiences.

Business: Informed Decision-Making and Efficiency

THE BUSINESS SECTOR also benefits significantly from the AI-IA synergy. Advanced analytics tools use AI to extract insights from vast quantities of business data, thereby augmenting decision-making processes. Tools like Tableau, which combines AI with intuitive visualization techniques, allow business leaders to make informed decisions quickly and confidently (Chen et al., 2018).

Additionally, IA tools enhance employee productivity by automating routine tasks, allowing the workforce to focus on more strategic and creative responsibilities. From patient bedsides to classrooms and corporate boardrooms, the integration of AI and IA is making waves, enhancing human capacity, and transforming how we diagnose diseases, educate our youth, and make business decisions. These case studies offer a promising glimpse into a future where AI and IA seamlessly merge, unlocking the next level of human potential.

Challenges in Synergizing AI and IA

THE MARRIAGE OF AI and IA, while powerful in its transformative potential, is not without its set of challenges. From technical and design obstacles to ethical and societal issues, the path to achieving an effective and harmonious AI-IA synergy is complex and winding. Yet, each challenge also provides an opportunity for innovation and improvement.

Technical and Design Challenges

ONE OF THE KEY TECHNICAL challenges lies in creating systems that effectively integrate AI's computational prowess with IA's human-centered approach. Achieving seamless interoperability between AI and IA systems is an ongoing challenge that requires continuous research and development (R&D) efforts (Norvig, Davis, & Russell, 2009).

Design challenges revolve around creating user-friendly interfaces that allow users to understand and interact with AI systems effectively. It is vital to ensure the design does not overwhelm the user with complexity or cause a cognitive overload, thereby maintaining IA's core principle of enhancing human cognitive capacities rather than hindering them (Norman, 2013).

Ethical and Societal Challenges

ON THE ETHICAL AND societal front, questions around data privacy, transparency, and the impact on employment loom large. AI and IA often involve collecting and analyzing vast amounts of data, raising privacy concerns (Bostrom & Yudkowsky, 2014). Furthermore, AI's often 'black-box' operations can be at odds with IA's emphasis on transparency, potentially causing distrust among users.

Overcoming Challenges: Proposed Strategies

TO NAVIGATE THESE CHALLENGES, a multipronged strategy is required. On the technical front, continued investment in R&D and fostering collaborations among industry, academia, and government can spur technological advancements.

For design challenges, adhering to user-centered design principles and incorporating user feedback throughout the design process can create more intuitive and accessible systems (Norman, 2013).

Addressing ethical and societal challenges requires a robust regulatory framework that safeguards privacy and fosters transparency. Furthermore, strategies such as re-skilling and lifelong learning can mitigate the potential employment impacts of AI and IA technologies (Arntz, Gregory, & Zierahn, 2016).

Despite the hurdles, the potential of AI-IA synergy offers a compelling call to action. By tackling these challenges head-on, we can move closer to realizing the full potential of AI and IA and charting a path toward a future where technology is a seamless extension of human capabilities.

Future Perspectives: The AI-IA Synergy

LOOKING AHEAD, THE AI-IA synergy promises to unveil a new frontier in cognitive technology. As we move forward into this thrilling landscape, let's consider some emerging trends, potential impacts, and future directions in the field.

Emerging Trends in AI-IA Integration

A SIGNIFICANT TREND in AI-IA integration is the move toward more transparent and explainable AI, reflecting IA's emphasis on transparency and human understanding. With the advent of Explainable AI (XAI), AI systems are becoming more transparent, providing understandable reasoning behind their decisions (Gunning, 2019).

In addition, the use of AI in augmenting creative capabilities is gaining traction. AI tools that provide creative assistance in fields like art, music, and writing point toward a future where AI enhances analytical capabilities and augments human creativity (Elgammal, Liu, Elhoseiny, & Mazzone, 2017).

Potential Impacts and Benefits of Deeper Integration

DEEPER INTEGRATION of AI and IA is set to bring about transformative impacts and benefits. With improved AI-IA systems, we can expect to see heightened productivity and efficiency across various sectors as machines handle routine tasks and humans focus on higher-order cognitive tasks.

Moreover, enhanced decision-making capabilities resulting from AI's advanced analytics combined with IA's focus on human cognition could lead to more informed decisions in healthcare and business fields (Norvig, Davis, & Russell, 2009).

Furthermore, as AI systems become more transparent and user-centered, public trust and acceptance of AI technologies will likely increase, paving the way for more widespread adoption and use of these technologies.

Future Research and Development Directions

FUTURE RESEARCH AND development efforts in AI-IA integration must address the key challenges discussed earlier. Continuous investment in R&D, interdisciplinary collaborations, and user-centric design approaches can drive technological advancements in the field.

Additionally, research efforts should focus on understanding and addressing AI-IA integration's societal and ethical implications. This includes studying the impact on employment, data privacy issues, and developing ethical guidelines along with robust regulatory frameworks.

As we look toward the future of AI-IA synergy, it's clear that our journey has just begun. By continuing to push the boundaries of what's possible, we can harness the power of AI and IA to create a future where humans and machines work in harmony, unlocking new realms of human potential.

Conclusion: The Transformative Potential of AI and IA Synergy

AS WE CLOSE THIS EXPLORATION into the synergy between AI and IA, let's pause to reflect on the journey and consider the transformative potential that lies at this exciting intersection of cognitive technologies.

Summary of Key Insights and Findings

WE'VE TRAVERSED THE vast terrain of AI and IA, observing their complementary roles in augmenting human intelligence and enhancing our abilities. We've witnessed their successful integration in various sectors, such as healthcare, education, and business, where their synergy has empowered more accurate diagnoses, personalized learning experiences, and informed business decisions.

However, the journey was not without its share of challenges. The road to achieving effective AI-IA integration presents a complex landscape, from technical and design hurdles to societal and ethical implications. Yet, each challenge brings opportunities for innovation and improvement, continuously pushing us to strive for better, more harmonious AI-IA systems.

Closing Thoughts on the AI-IA Synergy

THE SYNTHESIS OF AI and IA holds transformative potential. It promises a future where technology serves not as a replacement but as an amplifier of human potential, blending seamlessly with our cognitive processes to help us navigate an increasingly complex world. The journey toward this future is fraught with challenges, but each hurdle we overcome brings us one step closer to this vision.

Looking ahead, we must continue fostering an environment of research, collaboration, and innovation, focusing on user-centric design and ethical considerations. As we do so, we inch closer to realizing the promise of AI and IA—a world where humans and machines work in harmony, unlocking unprecedented levels of human potential.

While this chapter closes, the narrative of AI and IA continues, an ongoing saga of human ingenuity and technological advancement. And as we turn the page toward the future, it's clear that the best is yet to come.

References

ARNTZ, M., GREGORY, T., & Zierahn, U. (2016). The Risk of Automation for Jobs in OECD Countries: A Comparative Analysis. OECD Social, Employment and Migration Working Papers, No. 189, OECD Publishing, Paris.

Bostrom, N., & Yudkowsky, E. (2014). The Ethics of Artificial Intelligence. In K. Frankish & W. M. Ramsey (Eds.), The Cambridge Handbook of Artificial Intelligence (pp. 316-334). Cambridge: Cambridge University Press.

Chen, H., Chiang, R. H., & Storey, V. C. (2012). Business Intelligence and Analytics: From Big Data to Big Impact. MIS Quarterly, 36(4), 1165-1188.

Dilmurod, R., & Fazliddin, A. (2021). Prospects for the introduction of artificial intelligence technologies in higher education. ACADEMICIA: AN INTERNATIONAL MULTIDISCIPLINARY RESEARCH JOURNAL. https://doi.org/10.5958/2249-7137.2021.00468.7.

Elgammal, A., Liu, B., Elhoseiny, M., & Mazzone, M. (2017). CAN: Creative Adversarial Networks, Generating" Art" by Learning About Styles and Deviating from Style Norms. arXiv preprint arXiv:1706.07068.

Engelbart, D. C., & Friedewald, M. (1997). *Augmenting human intellect: A conceptual framework*. Stanford Research Institute.

Floridi, L., & Cowls, J. (2022). A unified framework of five principles for AI in society. *Machine learning and the city: Applications in architecture and urban design*, 535-545.

Gunning, D. (2019). Explainable Artificial Intelligence (XAI). Defense Advanced Research Projects Agency (DARPA), and Web, 2(2).

Kohli, M., & Tan, S. S. (2016). Electronic health records: how can IS researchers contribute to transforming healthcare? MIS Quarterly, 40(3), 553-573.

LeCun, Y., Bengio, Y., & Hinton, G. (2015). Deep learning. Nature, 521(7553), 436-444.

Norman, D. (2013). The Design of Everyday Things: Revised and Expanded Edition. Basic Books.

Norvig, P., Davis, E., Russell, S. J. (2009). Artificial Intelligence: A Modern Approach. United Kingdom: Prentice Hall.

Ribeiro, M. T., Singh, S., & Guestrin, C. (2016). "Why should I trust you?" Explaining the predictions of any classifier. In Proceedings of the 22nd ACM SIGKDD international conference on knowledge discovery and data mining (pp. 1135-1144).

Chapter 5: The Ethics of AI and IA

The Need for Ethical Considerations

AS WE EMBARK ON OUR exploration of the ethics surrounding Artificial Intelligence (AI) and Intelligence Augmentation (IA), we recognize a theme that has been threading through our journey so far: the necessity of considering the human element.

With their far-reaching implications, the ethical considerations of AI and IA are not just a philosophical contemplation but a critical and practical aspect of these technologies' development and application.

The Significance of Ethics in AI and IA

THE SIGNIFICANCE OF ethics in AI and IA cannot be overstated. These technologies are not just neutral tools but have the power to profoundly impact individuals and society, influencing our lives in ways ranging from the everyday mundane to major life decisions (Mittelstadt, Allo, Taddeo, Wachter, & Floridi, 2016). As AI algorithms make predictions, decisions, or take actions that affect humans, ethical issues around fairness, accountability, transparency, and privacy become crucial. Similarly, IA technologies, designed to augment human capabilities, raise substantial ethical questions. As they become integral to our decision-making processes, questions arise about responsibility, consent, and the equitable distribution of these enhancements (Michaelian & Arango-Muñoz, 2018).

Overview of Ethical Concerns

THE ETHICAL CONCERNS surrounding AI and IA are wide-ranging and multifaceted. They encompass areas such as:

- As AI and IA often rely on collecting and analyzing vast amounts of data, how do we protect personal information?

- Can we understand and explain how AI makes decisions, especially when complex machine learning algorithms are involved?
- How do we prevent AI systems from inheriting or amplifying existing human biases?
- When an AI or IA system makes a decision, who is responsible if something goes wrong?
- Who gets to benefit from AI and IA technologies? Are they accessible to everyone, or do they risk widening socio-economic disparities?

Ethical Implications of AI

THE ETHICAL IMPLICATIONS of Artificial Intelligence (AI) are profound and multifaceted, mirroring the transformative potential of this technology. As we navigate these ethical dimensions, we'll encounter some of the most pressing concerns when we imbue machines with intelligence.

Privacy and Data Security

IN THE AGE OF AI, DATA is the new oil—a vital resource that powers machine learning algorithms. However, collecting, storing, and analyzing vast amounts of data presents significant privacy and security challenges (Bostrom & Yudkowsky, 2014). While personalized AI services can enhance convenience, they often require access to sensitive personal information. How do we reconcile the need for data with the right to privacy? Moreover, ensuring data security is paramount as cyber threats become increasingly sophisticated.

Algorithmic Bias and Discrimination

ALGORITHMIC BIAS IS another critical ethical issue in AI. AI systems learn from data, and if this data reflects societal biases, the AI can unintentionally perpetuate or even amplify these biases (Buolamwini & Gebru, 2018). From facial recognition systems that misidentify certain ethnic groups to hiring algorithms that favor certain genders, the consequences of algorithmic bias can be far-reaching and discriminatory.

AI Autonomy and Accountability

AS AI SYSTEMS GAIN greater autonomy, questions around accountability become increasingly complex (Bryson & Winfield, 2017). When an autonomous AI makes a decision that leads to harm, who is responsible—the creator of the AI, the user, or the AI itself? These questions become even more critical as AI is integrated into high-stakes areas like autonomous vehicles or healthcare.

The Impact of AI on Jobs and Economic Inequality

AI'S IMPACT ON THE workforce and economic inequality is a pressing ethical concern. While AI can automate routine tasks, thereby increasing efficiency, it can also lead to job displacement. Moreover, the benefits of AI-driven economic growth may not be evenly distributed, potentially exacerbating income disparities (Chui, Manyika, & Miremadi, 2016). How do we ensure the transition to an AI-driven economy is inclusive and equitable?

Ethical Implications of IA

AS WE TURN OUR ATTENTION to Intelligence Augmentation (IA), we encounter different ethical challenges. While IA aims to enhance human intelligence and not replace it, its implications stretch into the realm of individual responsibility, privacy, access, and societal impacts.

Augmented Decision-Making and Responsibility

IA TECHNOLOGIES ENHANCE our decision-making ability by providing valuable insights and analyses. However, as we rely more on these systems, questions arise about responsibility and accountability. Who bears the responsibility when a decision, guided by IA, goes awry (Turilli & Floridi, 2009)? While IA is intended to augment rather than substitute human judgment, these questions pose serious ethical dilemmas.

Privacy and IA

MUCH LIKE AI, IA TECHNOLOGIES also raise significant privacy concerns. IA systems often require access to personal data to provide personalized services and augmentations. Moreover, as these systems become more embedded in our lives, they can potentially intrude into our personal space, thus raising concerns about privacy and consent (Mittelstadt, Allo, Taddeo, Wachter, & Floridi, 2016).

Access to IA Technology and Digital Divide Issues

ACCESS TO IA TECHNOLOGIES is not evenly distributed, and this digital divide presents significant ethical challenges. While IA holds the potential to enhance human abilities significantly, its benefits are currently skewed toward those who can afford these technologies. How do we ensure the benefits of IA are accessible to all, thereby preventing the augmentation gap from exacerbating existing socio-economic disparities? (Michaelian, & Arango-Muñoz, 2018)

Cognitive Enhancements and Societal Implications

IA TECHNOLOGIES, ESPECIALLY those providing cognitive enhancements, bring about societal implications. They may change how we perceive human intelligence and what we value in education and work. Furthermore, the widespread use of cognitive enhancements may change societal expectations, potentially pressuring individuals into using augmentations to keep up (Sparrow, 2014).

As we navigate the ethical landscape of IA, these questions guide our exploration, encouraging a thoughtful and informed approach to IA's integration into society.

Case Studies: Ethical Issues in AI and IA Applications

LET'S DELVE INTO REAL-world applications to further understand the ethical implications of AI and IA. Through case studies in healthcare, finance, and social media, we'll explore the ethical challenges that emerge when AI and IA are integrated into different facets of society.

Healthcare

AI AND IA ARE REVOLUTIONIZING healthcare, from AI algorithms that predict disease outbreaks to IA tools that support clinical decision-making (Topol, 2019). However, these advancements bring ethical issues. For instance, patient data used to train AI systems raise privacy concerns. There's also the question of accountability— if an AI tool provides incorrect or misleading information, leading to a misdiagnosis, who is responsible? And when IA tools augment the decision-making process, there is a need to ensure they support rather than override the professional judgment of healthcare providers.

Finance

IN THE FINANCE SECTOR, AI is used for everything from risk assessment to fraud detection, while IA tools assist in making complex investment decisions (Arner, Barberis, & Buckley, 2016). The ethical concerns here revolve around fairness and transparency.

AI systems making credit decisions could inadvertently discriminate against certain groups if the training data reflects societal biases. And the transparency of IA-supported decisions becomes critical when financial advisors use these tools, as customers have the right to understand how advice is formulated.

Social Media and Digital Platforms

AI AND IA HAVE SIGNIFICANT roles in social media and digital platforms, influencing what content we see and shaping our online interactions (Gillespie, 2014). Here, the ethical concerns range from filter bubbles, which can limit exposure to diverse viewpoints, to privacy concerns related to data collection practices. Moreover, AI-driven content moderation has been criticized for failing to catch harmful content and suppressing freedom of expression. These case studies highlight that while AI and IA have enormous potential, their implementation is fraught with ethical challenges. They remind us that robust ethical frameworks must guide the advancement of these technologies to ensure their benefits are realized without compromising our values.

Developing Ethical Guidelines for AI and IA

GIVEN THE PROFOUND ethical implications of AI and IA, it is critical to have robust ethical guidelines and regulations governing their development and use. Let's explore existing ethical frameworks, consider ethical AI and IA principles, and discuss the role of regulation and policy.

Existing Ethical Frameworks and Guidelines

SEVERAL ORGANIZATIONS have proposed ethical guidelines for AI and IA. For instance, the IEEE has published *Ethically Aligned Design,* which outlines principles for ensuring AI and autonomous systems prioritize human well-being (Shahriari & Shahriari, 2017). Similarly, the Partnership on AI, a collaboration among major tech companies and non-profits, focuses on creating a shared understanding of best practices in AI technologies (Partnership on AI, 2019). These efforts underline the growing consensus on the importance of ethical considerations in AI and IA.

Principles for Ethical AI and IA

SEVERAL KEY PRINCIPLES emerge as central to ethical AI and IA. These include: transparency—ensuring AI and IA systems operate in ways that are understandable and interpretable, fairness—preventing biases from being built into AI and IA systems, privacy—protecting personal data utilized by AI and IA systems, and accountability—identifying who is responsible when things go wrong (Floridi et al., 2021).

The Role of Regulation and Policy

WHILE ETHICAL GUIDELINES set the stage for responsible AI and IA development, their implementation often relies on effective regulation and policy. Regulatory bodies and governments worldwide are grappling with creating policies that balance the benefits of AI and IA with potential risks. Regulation can provide legal frameworks to enforce ethical guidelines, protect individuals, and ensure that companies are held accountable (Cath, Wachter, Mittelstadt, Taddeo, & Floridi, 2018).

In the future, fostering an ethical AI and IA ecosystem will require a collaborative effort involving technologists, ethicists, policy-makers, and society at large. It will be a continual process, evolving alongside these transformative technologies.

Conclusion: Navigating Ethical Dilemmas in AI and IA

AS WE CONCLUDE OUR exploration of the ethical dimensions of AI and IA, we are left with an awareness of the critical need for careful navigation of this dynamic landscape. Despite the challenges and dilemmas, the power of AI and IA offers tremendous opportunities to enhance our lives, provided we approach them with thoughtful and responsible stewardship.

Key Takeaways and Insights

OUR JOURNEY THROUGH the ethical dimensions of AI and IA has presented us with several key insights. The application of these technologies raises numerous ethical considerations, from questions of accountability and transparency to issues of privacy and fairness. Different industries, from healthcare to social media, grapple with these concerns in their unique contexts.

Existing ethical frameworks and guidelines provide a foundation for navigating these challenges. Principles such as transparency, fairness, privacy, and accountability are key to ethical AI and IA development. Regulation and policy play an essential role in enforcing these principles, requiring a collective effort from technologists, ethicists, policy-makers, and society at large.

Looking Ahead: The Future of Ethical AI and IA

LOOKING AHEAD, THE future of AI and IA is as much about ethical evolution as it is about technological advancement. As these technologies continue to grow in power and influence, our ethical understanding and frameworks must evolve alongside them.

The challenges of ensuring ethical AI and IA are daunting, yet they also represent an opportunity. By addressing these challenges, we can guide the development of AI and IA in a way that respects our values and enhances our lives. We stand at the cusp of a future where AI and IA are integral parts of our lives—let's ensure we step into this future with our ethical compass firmly in hand.

References

ARNER, D. W., BARBERIS, J. N., & Buckley, R. P. (2016). The Evolution of FinTech: A New Post-Crisis Paradigm? Georgetown Journal of International Law, 47(4), 1271-1319.

Bostrom, N., & Yudkowsky, E. (2014). The Ethics of Artificial Intelligence. In K. Frankish & W. M. Ramsey (Eds.), The Cambridge Handbook of Artificial Intelligence (pp. 316-334). Cambridge: Cambridge University Press.

Bryson, J., & Winfield, A. (2017). Standardizing Ethical Design for Artificial Intelligence and Autonomous Systems. Computer, 50(5), 116-119.

Buolamwini, J., & Gebru, T. (2018). Gender Shades: Intersectional Accuracy Disparities in Commercial Gender Classification. Proceedings of the Machine Learning Research, 81, 1-15.

Cath, C., Wachter, S., Mittelstadt, B., Taddeo, M., & Floridi, L. (2018). Artificial Intelligence and the 'Good Society': the US, EU, and UK approach. Science and engineering ethics, 24(2), 505-528.

Chui, M., Manyika, J., & Miremadi, M. (2016). Where machines could replace humans—and where they can't (yet). McKinsey Quarterly.

Floridi, L., Cowls, J., Beltrametti, M., Chatila, R., Chazerand, P., Dignum, V., ... & Vayena, E. (2021). An ethical framework for a good AI society: Opportunities, risks, principles, and recommendations. *Ethics, governance, and policies in artificial intelligence*, 19-39.

Gillespie, T. (2014). The Relevance of Algorithms. In Media Technologies: Essays on Communication, Materiality, and Society (pp. 167–194). MIT Press.

Michaelian, K., & Arango-Muñoz, S. (2018). Collaborative memory knowledge: A distributed reliabilist perspective.

Mittelstadt, B. D., Allo, P., Taddeo, M., Wachter, S., & Floridi, L. (2016). The ethics of algorithms: Mapping the debate. *Big Data & Society*, 3(2), 2053951716679679.

Mittelstadt, B., Allo, P., Taddeo, M., Wachter, S., & Floridi, L. (2016). The ethics of algorithms: Mapping the debate. Big Data & Society, 3(2), 205395171667967.

Partnership on AI. (2019). Partnership on AI Update: Building the Partnership. Partnership on AI. Retrieved from: https://partnershiponai.org/

Shahriari, K., & Shahriari, M. (2017, July). IEEE standard review—Ethically aligned design: A vision for prioritizing human wellbeing with artificial intelligence and autonomous systems. In *2017 IEEE Canada International Humanitarian Technology Conference (IHTC)* (pp. 197-201). IEEE.

Sparrow, R. (2014). Better Living Through Chemistry? A Reply to Savulescu and Persson on 'Moral Enhancement.' Journal of Applied Philosophy, 31(1), 23–32.

Topol, E. J. (2019). High-performance medicine: the convergence of human and artificial intelligence. Nature Medicine, 25(1), 44–56.

Turilli, M., & Floridi, L. (2009). The Ethics of Information Transparency. Ethics and Information Technology, 11(2), 105–112.

Chapter 6: AI and IA in Healthcare

AI and IA in the Context of Healthcare

THE ADVENT OF ARTIFICIAL Intelligence (AI) and Intelligence Augmentation (IA) has brought a paradigm shift in numerous sectors, and healthcare is no exception. With their potential to transform diagnosis, treatment, patient care, and management, these technologies are increasingly becoming integral parts of the healthcare ecosystem.

The Role of AI and IA in Healthcare

THE ROLE OF AI AND IA in healthcare is multifaceted and transformative. With its ability to analyze vast amounts of data and identify patterns beyond human capacity, AI has proven to be a game-changer in areas such as diagnosis, predictive analytics, and personalized medicine. From aiding in the early detection of diseases to assisting in complex surgeries, AI is opening up new frontiers in medical science (Jiang et al., 2017).

Simultaneously, IA is a powerful ally to healthcare professionals, augmenting human capabilities rather than replacing them. It provides tools to enhance the decision-making process, support patient monitoring, improve workflow efficiency, and elevate patient engagement in their care (Bodenstedt et al., 2020).

Potential and Existing Applications in Healthcare

THE APPLICATIONS OF AI and IA in healthcare are numerous and continue to expand. AI has been leveraged in imaging diagnostics to identify diseases with remarkable accuracy, surpassing even expert clinicians in some instances. It has also significantly contributed to predicting patient risks, allowing for proactive intervention rather than reactive treatment (Topol, 2019). On the other hand, IA applications have empowered patients to take charge of their health through wearable devices, mobile health applications, and telemedicine platforms. By augmenting the ability of healthcare providers to deliver care, these technologies have made it possible to extend medical services into the home and beyond traditional healthcare settings (Steinhubl, Muse, & Topol, 2015).

In the intersection of AI and IA lies a wealth of opportunities to redefine the boundaries of healthcare, creating a high-tech and high-touch environment, augmenting human capabilities while preserving the personal, human elements at the heart of healthcare.

AI in Healthcare

ARTIFICIAL INTELLIGENCE (AI) holds immense promise for transforming healthcare as we know it. By providing the ability to analyze and interpret vast amounts of data quickly, AI can aid in many areas, from disease diagnosis and prognosis to treatment planning and healthcare management.

AI in Disease Diagnosis and Prognosis

AI HAS SHOWN EXTRAORDINARY potential in disease diagnosis and prognosis. Machine learning algorithms are being used to analyze imaging data and detect abnormalities, sometimes with higher accuracy than human experts. For instance, AI algorithms have been used to diagnose skin cancer by analyzing skin images and to predict the progression of diseases such as Alzheimer's by assessing brain scans (Esteva et al., 2017; Korolev et al., 2017).

In addition, AI can analyze electronic health records and use predictive modeling to anticipate disease progression, allowing clinicians to intervene earlier and potentially alter the course of the disease (Rajkomar et al., 2018).

AI in Treatment Planning and Personalized Medicine

AI ALSO PLAYS A CRUCIAL role in treatment planning and personalized medicine. By analyzing a patient's unique genetic makeup and other health data, AI can help identify an individual's most effective treatment plan, optimizing outcomes and reducing side effects. Companies like Tempus are leveraging AI to create personalized therapeutic approaches for cancer patients (Krittanawong et al., 2020).

AI in Healthcare Management and Operations

BEYOND DIRECT PATIENT care, AI is proving useful in managing healthcare operations. From optimizing staff scheduling to predictive medical equipment maintenance, AI can improve efficiency and reduce costs. AI is also playing a crucial role in health informatics, aiding in managing and analyzing health data to improve healthcare services and outcomes (Bresnick, 2018).

As we continue to explore the capabilities of AI in healthcare, we can look forward to a future of improved disease prediction, personalized treatment plans, and more efficient healthcare systems, all underpinned by the power of artificial intelligence.

IA in Healthcare

WHILE AI BRINGS THE power of automation and predictive analytics to healthcare, Intelligence Augmentation (IA) opens up a different yet complementary avenue for transformation. IA stands on the premise of augmenting human intelligence with the help of technology, ensuring that the human touch remains at the core of healthcare delivery.

IA in Supporting Clinicians and Healthcare Professionals

IA PROVIDES TOOLS AND technologies designed to enhance the capabilities of clinicians and healthcare professionals. These tools can provide timely and relevant information, aiding in decision-making processes. For instance, Clinical Decision Support Systems (CDSS) employ IA to provide real-time diagnostic assistance, flag potential drug interactions, and suggest appropriate treatment plans, thereby enhancing the quality of care and reducing errors (Bates et al., 2014).

IA in Patient Engagement and Self-Management

THROUGH IA, PATIENTS are empowered to participate more actively in their health management. For example, wearable devices and health apps enable continuous monitoring of vital signs and encourage healthier lifestyles. Interactive platforms and telehealth services augment the traditional patient-doctor relationship, fostering more effective communication and engagement (Swan, 2012).

IA in Medical Research and Drug Discovery

IA ALSO PLAYS A CRITICAL role in medical research and drug discovery. It can aid researchers in synthesizing and analyzing vast amounts of data, identifying patterns and insights that could lead to novel therapeutic strategies. Tools like IBM's Watson for Drug Discovery employ IA to analyze and interpret scientific literature, genetic data, and molecular databases, significantly accelerating the pace of research and discovery (Chen et al., 2016).

As we continue to harness the potential of IA in healthcare, we pave the way for a future where technology serves as an ally to human intelligence, not a substitute. The result is a healthcare landscape where the human element remains central, supported, and enhanced by intelligent technology.

Case Studies: Successful Implementation of AI and IA in Healthcare

ACROSS THE HEALTHCARE sector, AI and IA have been put to work, revolutionizing patient care, diagnosis, and treatment. Let's explore some fields where these technologies have profoundly impacted: oncology, mental health, and telemedicine.

AI and IA in Oncology

IN ONCOLOGY, AI AND IA have demonstrated immense potential. AI algorithms, such as those developed by Tempus, can analyze a patient's genetic data and use it to suggest personalized treatment plans, transforming the fight against cancer (Krittanawong et al., 2017). On the other hand, IA tools like IBM's Watson for Oncology assist physicians by providing evidence-backed treatment recommendations, augmenting the physician's expertise, and ensuring that patients receive the best possible care (Kohli & Tan, 2016).

AI and IA in Mental Health

THE MENTAL HEALTH FIELD has also seen transformative effects from AI and IA. AI algorithms can analyze a person's speech, text, or social media activity to detect signs of mental health conditions, enabling early intervention (Birnbaum et al., 2017). However, IA has given rise to various therapeutic tools and apps that provide cognitive behavioral therapy, augmenting traditional mental health treatments and making therapy more accessible (Firth et al., 2017).

AI and IA in Telemedicine

IN TELEMEDICINE, THE combination of AI and IA is reshaping healthcare delivery. AI can aid in remote patient monitoring, predictive analytics, and triage, ensuring patients receive timely care. Through teleconsultation platforms, IA enhances patient-doctor communication, enabling the delivery of healthcare services irrespective of geographical distances (Hollander & Carr, 2020).

As we continue exploring the intersections of AI and IA in healthcare, these case studies serve as a testament to the transformative potential these technologies hold, reshaping the healthcare landscape and amplifying human intelligence at every step.

Challenges and Ethical Considerations

WHILE AI AND IA HAVE the potential to revolutionize healthcare, they also bring forth a host of challenges and ethical considerations. Data privacy, algorithmic bias, and ethical decision-making stand out as some of the most critical concerns in this domain.

Data Privacy and Security

THE USE OF AI AND IA in healthcare often requires collecting and analyzing sensitive patient data. Ensuring the privacy and security of this data is paramount (Rumbold & Pierscionek, 2017). Healthcare providers must implement robust security measures to protect against data breaches. Furthermore, the use of patient data must adhere to regulations such as the General Data Protection Regulation (GDPR) in Europe or the Health Insurance Portability and Accountability Act (HIPAA) in the United States.

Algorithmic Bias and Fairness

AI SYSTEMS LEARN FROM data, and if this data contains biases, the AI system can inadvertently perpetuate or exacerbate these biases. In healthcare, this could lead to unequal or unfair treatment of patients. To address this issue, it is important to ensure the data used to train AI systems is representative and unbiased and that the systems themselves are regularly audited for fairness (Rajkomar et al., 2018).

Ethical Implications of AI and IA in Healthcare Decision-making

AI AND IA TECHNOLOGIES augment human decision-making in healthcare. However, there are concerns about accountability and the 'dehumanization' of care. The final decision-making power should rest with human professionals, ensuring that machines augment, rather than replace, human judgment (Vayena et al., 2018).

As we continue to harness AI and IA in healthcare, we must navigate these challenges with care and consideration, ensuring the technology we build is secure, fair, and ethically grounded.

Future of AI and IA in Healthcare

THE BURGEONING FIELDS of AI and IA hold much promise for the future of healthcare. From advancing personalized medicine to redefining patient care, the potential impacts are profound and far-reaching.

Emerging Trends and Technologies

SEVERAL EMERGING TRENDS indicate the future trajectory of AI and IA in healthcare. Among them, the rise of predictive analytics for patient risk stratification, the use of AI in genomic analysis for personalized treatments, and the integration of AI and IA in wearable and implantable technologies for continuous patient monitoring are noteworthy (Topol, 2019).

Anticipated Impacts on Healthcare Providers and Patients

THE APPLICATION OF AI and IA is poised to significantly alter the healthcare landscape. For providers, these technologies can aid in diagnosis, treatment planning, and patient management, thereby increasing efficiency and reducing burnout. For patients, AI and IA offer the promise of personalized, efficient care, greater engagement in their health management, and improved health outcomes (Jiang et al., 2017).

Future Research and Development Directions

DESPITE CONSIDERABLE progress, there is much to explore in the realm of AI and IA in healthcare. Future research should focus on refining algorithms for better accuracy, devising strategies to ensure the ethical use of these technologies, and conducting large-scale, real-world studies to evaluate their impact on patient outcomes (Wiens et al., 2019).

The fusion of AI and IA is not just about technological advancement. It is about shaping a healthcare future where technology serves humanity, augmenting our abilities, and creating systems that understand and adapt to our needs.

Conclusion: The Promise of AI and IA in Transforming Healthcare

AS WE DRAW THE CURTAIN on this deep dive into the role of AI and IA in healthcare, the transformational potential of these technologies becomes undeniably clear.

Key Takeaways and Insights

AI AND IA ARE PROVING to be formidable allies in our quest for improved healthcare. They have shown immense promise in enhancing the precision of diagnosis, personalizing treatment planning, optimizing healthcare management, and redefining patient care. However, their application is not without challenges, and these technologies necessitate serious ethical considerations, particularly in data privacy, algorithmic bias, and decision-making.

Final Thoughts on the Potential of AI and IA in Healthcare

THE ONGOING FUSION of AI and IA in healthcare paints a picture of a future where technology is deeply intertwined with our pursuit of better health. It imagines a future where machines don't replace humans but work alongside them, enhancing their capabilities and intuition.

AUGMENTING INTELLIGENCE, THE SYNERGY BETWEEN ARTIFICIAL INTELLIGENCE AND INTELLIGENCE AUGMENTATION

This is not to say that the journey will be easy. The path to fully integrating AI and IA in healthcare will require careful navigation, balancing technological advancements with ethical considerations, and ensuring the human element remains central in this digital transformation.

In the words of William J. Mayo, "The aim of medicine is to prevent disease and prolong life. The ideal of medicine is to eliminate the need for a physician." In their capacity to augment human abilities and democratize healthcare, AI and IA bring us closer to this ideal.

In the end, perhaps the greatest promise of AI and IA in healthcare is their potential to make healthcare a more human, empathetic, and accessible service, transforming it from a reactive to a proactive force for good.

References

BATES, D. W., SARIA, S., Ohno-Machado, L., Shah, A., & Escobar, G. (2014). Big data in health care: using analytics to identify and manage high-risk and high-cost patients. Health Affairs, 33(7), 1123-1131.

Birnbaum, M. L., Rizvi, A. F., Confino, J., Correll, C. U., & Kane, J. M. (2017). Role of social media and the Internet in pathways to care for adolescents and young adults with psychotic disorders and non-psychotic mood disorders. Early intervention in psychiatry, 11(4), 290-295.

Bodenstedt, S., Wagner, M., Müller-Stich, B., Weitz, J., & Speidel, S. (2020). Artificial Intelligence-Assisted Surgery: Potential and Challenges. Visceral Medicine, 36, 450 - 455. https://doi.org/10.1159/000511351.

Bresnick, J. (2018). Top 12 Ways Artificial Intelligence Will Impact Healthcare. HealthITAnalytics. Retrieved from https://healthitanalytics.com/news/top-12-ways-artificial-intelligence-will-impact-healthcare.

Chen, Y., Argentinis, J. E., & Weber, G. (2016). IBM Watson: how cognitive computing can be applied to big data challenges in life sciences research. *Clinical therapeutics*, 38(4), 688-701.

Esteva, A., Kuprel, B., Novoa, R. A., Ko, J., Swetter, S. M., Blau, H. M., & Thrun, S. (2017). Dermatologist-level classification of skin cancer with deep neural networks. Nature, 542(7639), 115-118.

Firth, J., Torous, J., Nicholas, J., Carney, R., Pratap, A., Rosenbaum, S., & Sarris, J. (2017). The efficacy of smartphone-based mental health interventions for depressive symptoms: a meta-analysis of randomized controlled trials. World psychiatry, 16(3), 287-298.

Hollander, J. E., & Carr, B. G. (2020). Virtually perfect? Telemedicine for Covid-19. The New England journal of medicine, 382(18), 1679-1681.

Jiang, F., Jiang, Y., Zhi, H., Dong, Y., Li, H., Ma, S., ... & Wang, Y. (2017). Artificial intelligence in healthcare: past, present and future. Stroke and Vascular Neurology, 2(4), 230-243.

Jiang, F., Jiang, Y., Zhi, H., Dong, Y., Li, H., Ma, S., Wang, Y., Dong, Q., Shen, H., & Wang, Y. (2017). Artificial intelligence in healthcare: past, present and future. Stroke and Vascular Neurology, 2(4), 230–243.

Kohli, M., & Tan, S. S. (2016). Electronic health records: how can IS researchers contribute to transforming healthcare? MIS Quarterly, 40(3), 553-573

Korolev, S., Safiullin, A., Belyaev, M., & Dodonova, Y. (2017, April). Residual and plain convolutional neural networks for 3D brain MRI classification. In *2017 IEEE 14th international symposium on biomedical imaging (ISBI 2017)* (pp. 835-838). IEEE.

Krittanawong, C., Zhang, H., Wang, Z., Aydar, M., & Kitai, T. (2017). Artificial intelligence in precision cardiovascular medicine. *Journal of the American College of Cardiology*, 69(21), 2657-2664.

Krittanawong, C., Zhang, H., Wang, Z., Aydar, M., & Kitai, T. (2017). Artificial intelligence in precision cardiovascular medicine. *Journal of the American College of Cardiology*, 69(21), 2657-2664.

Rajkomar, A., Hardt, M., Howell, M. D., Corrado, G., & Chin, M. H. (2018). Ensuring fairness in machine learning to advance health equity. Annals of internal medicine, 169(12), 866-872.

Rajkomar, A., Oren, E., Chen, K., Dai, A. M., Hajaj, N., Hardt, M., ... & Sundberg, P. (2018). Scalable and accurate deep learning with electronic health records. NPJ Digital Medicine, 1(1), 1-10.

Rumbold, J. M. M., & Pierscionek, B. K. (2017). The effect of the General Data Protection Regulation on medical research. Journal of medical Internet research, 19(2), e47.

Steinhubl, S. R., Muse, E. D., & Topol, E. J. (2015). The emerging field of mobile health. Science translational medicine, 7(283), 283rv3-283rv3.

Swan, M. (2012). Health 2050: The realization of personalized medicine through crowdsourcing, the Quantified Self, and the participatory biocitizen. Journal of personalized medicine, 2(3), 93-118.

Topol, E. (2019). High-performance medicine: the convergence of human and artificial intelligence. Nature Medicine, 25, 44–56.

Topol, E. J. (2019). High-performance medicine: the convergence of human and artificial intelligence. Nature Medicine, 25(1), 44–56.

Vayena, E., Blasimme, A., & Cohen, I. G. (2018). Machine learning in medicine: Addressing ethical challenges. PLoS Medicine, 15(11), e1002689.

Wiens, J., Saria, S., Sendak, M., Ghassemi, M., Liu, V. X., Doshi-Velez, F., Jung, K., Heller, K., Kale, D., Saeed, M., Ossorio, P. N., Thadaney-Israni, S., & Goldenberg, A. (2019). Do no harm: a roadmap for responsible machine learning for health care. Nature Medicine, 25, 1337–1340.

Chapter 7: The Ethical and Regulatory Challenges in Integrating AI and IA in Healthcare Introduction

Ethics and Regulation in Healthcare

NAVIGATING THE COMPLEXITY of healthcare has always necessitated a compass, and ethics and regulation have long served this purpose. They offer us vital guidelines on our path toward healthcare innovation and help us ensure that this innovation serves humanity fairly, respectfully, and beneficially.

The Importance of Ethics and Regulation in Healthcare

ETHICS FORMS THE BACKBONE of healthcare, a field deeply intertwined with human life, dignity, and well-being (Morrison, 2016). It guides decisions that healthcare professionals make daily, influencing how we care for the sick, protect patient information, and ensure fair access to healthcare resources. Regulation, on the other hand, is the guardrail that ensures the safe, effective, and equitable operation of health systems (Field, 2006).

It provides legal frameworks to implement ethical principles, protect patient rights, and manage the quality and safety of healthcare services.

Specific Challenges Posed by AI and IA

THE ADVENT OF AI AND IA in healthcare, while promising transformative potential, also introduces unique ethical and regulatory challenges. For instance, the black-box nature of some AI algorithms can obscure the reasoning behind their decisions, raising questions about transparency and accountability (Char et al., 2018).

The vast amounts of data these technologies use also raise concerns about patient privacy and data security (Price & Cohen, 2019). Regulation of these technologies, too, is a complex task, requiring a fine balance between promoting innovation and ensuring safety and efficacy.

As we stand at the cusp of this AI and IA-driven healthcare revolution, it is paramount that we understand and address these challenges, weaving ethical and regulatory considerations into the fabric of this transformation.

Ethical Challenges in Integrating AI and IA in Healthcare

INTEGRATING AI AND IA in healthcare presents an exciting frontier with possibilities. However, this technological leap also brings with it a host of ethical challenges that we must navigate wisely.

Data Privacy and Confidentiality

AI AND IA SYSTEMS OFTEN require access to vast amounts of personal and medical data to function optimally (Mittelstadt et al., 2016). In the hands of healthcare providers, this data can lead to unprecedented insights and improved patient care. However, there is a pressing need to ensure that this data exchange does not compromise patient privacy and confidentiality.

Ethical frameworks must guide the collection, storage, and utilization of health data, ensuring compliance with standards like the Health Insurance Portability and Accountability Act (HIPAA) and the General Data Protection Regulation (GDPR).

Bias and Discrimination in AI and IA Algorithms

ANOTHER CONCERN IS the risk of bias and discrimination. AI and IA systems are only as good as the data they're trained on. If the training data reflects societal biases, these systems may perpetuate or even amplify those biases, leading to unfair outcomes in healthcare (Obermeyer et al., 2019). Ethical guidelines must promote fairness and equality in AI and IA systems, guiding the choice of training data and evaluating these systems' decisions.

Autonomy and the Human Touch in Healthcare

AI AND IA ALSO POSE ethical questions about balancing human and machine roles in healthcare. On the one hand, these technologies can extend the capabilities of healthcare professionals, allowing them to care for more patients effectively. On the other hand, over-reliance on technology could threaten the human touch in healthcare – the empathy, understanding, and personal connection that lie at the heart of the healing process (Meskó et al., 2018). We must strike a balance, harnessing the power of AI and IA without eroding the human essence of healthcare.

Regulatory Challenges in Integrating AI and IA in Healthcare

AS WE USHER IN AN ERA of AI and IA in healthcare, regulatory bodies worldwide are grappling with the task of crafting appropriate regulatory frameworks. These challenges are multi-faceted, revolving around the technical aspects of these technologies and their societal implications.

Challenges in Defining and Implementing Regulatory Standards

ONE OF THE FUNDAMENTAL challenges in regulating AI and IA technologies in healthcare is defining appropriate standards. AI and IA applications vary widely in their complexity, purpose, and risk profile. Determining what constitutes 'safe' and 'effective' for such a diverse array of technologies is complex (Gerke et al., 2020).

Furthermore, implementing these standards requires building robust mechanisms for testing, validation, and post-market surveillance of AI and IA technologies.

International Variation in AI and IA Regulation

ANOTHER CHALLENGE LIES in the international variation in regulatory frameworks for AI and IA in healthcare. Different countries have different standards, guidelines, and approaches to regulation. This can make it challenging for developers and users of AI and IA technologies to navigate regulatory compliance, particularly for technologies intended for international markets (Minssen et al., 2020).

Keeping Pace with Rapidly Evolving Technologies

PERHAPS THE MOST SIGNIFICANT challenge is the pace at which AI and IA technologies evolve. Regulatory bodies traditionally operate on timelines that can't keep up with the rapid advancement of these technologies (Rahimzadeh et al., 2018). This lag can lead to outdated regulations that fail to account for recent developments or, conversely, to regulatory gaps that leave new technologies unregulated. Addressing this challenge requires regulatory innovation, including mechanisms to update regulations dynamically as technology evolves.

Case Studies: Navigating Ethical and Regulatory Challenges

THE LANDSCAPE OF AI and IA in healthcare is fraught with ethical and regulatory challenges. Therefore, it is necessary to dive into case studies that highlight these complexities and offer lessons on navigating them.

Case Study 1: A Data Privacy Controversy

IN 2016, THE ROYAL Free NHS Foundation Trust in the UK entered into a data-sharing agreement with Google's DeepMind to develop an AI system for detecting kidney injury. However, the project soon came under scrutiny when it was revealed that the data of 1.6 million patients had been shared without their direct consent, sparking a major controversy around data privacy (Powles & Hodson, 2017).

The case highlighted the delicate balance between utilizing healthcare data for AI development and respecting patients' privacy rights, reinforcing the importance of transparent data governance practices.

Case Study 2: Addressing Bias in a Health AI System

A 2019 STUDY FOUND that a widely used healthcare risk prediction algorithm exhibited significant racial bias (Obermeyer et al., 2019). The AI system was designed to predict which patients would benefit from additional care, but it consistently underestimated the risk for Black patients, thereby influencing their access to care programs. This case underlined the critical need for rigorous testing and validation to ensure that AI systems do not perpetuate societal biases.

Case Study 3: Regulatory Hurdles in Launching an AI Diagnostic Tool

IN 2018, THE U.S. FDA approved the first AI-powered diagnostic device that provides screening decisions without needing a clinician's interpretation (U.S. FDA, 2018). The device, IDx-DR, uses AI to analyze images of the eye to detect diabetic retinopathy, a form of eye disease. The approval process posed unique regulatory challenges, requiring the FDA to evaluate an autonomous system that makes decisions independently of healthcare providers. The case provides insights into the regulatory complexities associated with autonomous AI systems in healthcare.

Ethical Frameworks and Regulatory Strategies for AI and IA in Healthcare

NAVIGATING THE ETHICAL and regulatory challenges associated with AI and IA in healthcare requires a comprehensive and balanced approach.

Proposed Ethical Frameworks for AI and IA in Healthcare

SEVERAL ETHICAL FRAMEWORKS have been proposed to guide the development and use of AI and IA in healthcare. These frameworks often highlight principles such as transparency, accountability, fairness, respect for human autonomy, and beneficence (Mittelstadt et al., 2016). These principles aim to ensure that AI and IA technologies are used in ways that respect human values, protect patient rights, and promote health and well-being.

The World Health Organization, for example, emphasizes a human rights-based approach to AI and IA in healthcare, calling for these technologies to be used in ways that respect the right to health, the right to privacy, and other fundamental human rights (WHO, 2021).

Strategies for Effective Regulation

EFFECTIVE REGULATION of AI and IA in healthcare requires strategies that can address the unique challenges posed by these technologies. These strategies may include the development of regulatory standards for AI and IA systems, establishing regulatory bodies to oversee their use, and creating mechanisms for testing and validating these technologies (Paton & Kobayashi, 2019).

The FDA's proposed regulatory framework for AI and machine learning-based Software as a Medical Device (SaMD) is one example of such strategies. This framework includes provisions for a "total product lifecycle" approach that allows modifications to be made to AI and machine learning algorithms while ensuring their safety and effectiveness (FDA, 2021).

Balancing Innovation and Accountability

BALANCING THE NEED for innovation with the need for accountability is a critical challenge in the regulation of AI and IA in healthcare. While we must encourage developing and adopting these potentially transformative technologies, we must also ensure they are used responsibly and do not harm patients or exacerbate health inequalities.

Striking this balance requires a nuanced approach that recognizes AI and IA's potential benefits and risks, promotes transparency and accountability, and encourages ongoing dialogue among stakeholders, including healthcare providers, patients, developers, and policymakers (Cohen et al., 2014).

Conclusion: Navigating the Path Forward

REFLECTING ON THE ETHICAL and regulatory challenges associated with AI and IA in healthcare, it becomes clear that navigating the path forward is as much a human endeavor as a technological one. As AI and IA continue to evolve, the ethical and regulatory landscapes will need to evolve with them in a dance that balances the desire for innovation with the necessity of responsibility.

Key Takeaways from Ethical and Regulatory Challenges

THE KEY TAKEAWAYS FROM our discussion can be summarized as follows:

- The ethical challenges AI and IA present in healthcare center around privacy, bias, discrimination, and human autonomy. We must continually question how these technologies can respect and uphold our shared human values even as they transform healthcare delivery.
- Regulatory challenges involve developing and implementing regulatory standards that keep pace with rapidly evolving technologies. While AI and IA offer promising opportunities to improve healthcare, they also pose risks that must be managed through thoughtful regulation.
- Case studies reveal real-world implications of these challenges and illustrate the need for ongoing vigilance, engagement, and dialogue among all stakeholders.
- Various ethical frameworks and regulatory strategies can guide us as we navigate these challenges. A balance between innovation and accountability is necessary to ensure that the benefits of AI and IA in healthcare can be realized without undue harm.

Looking Forward: Future Ethical and Regulatory Considerations for AI and IA in Healthcare

THE INTEGRATION OF AI and IA into healthcare will likely continue to raise new ethical and regulatory challenges. As AI and IA technologies become more sophisticated, issues such as the explainability of AI decisions, the equitable distribution of AI and IA benefits, and the potential for AI and IA to reshape the healthcare profession will gain importance.

In addition, as AI and IA technologies are adopted globally, international cooperation will be needed to address ethical and regulatory challenges that transcend national borders.

The path forward may be complex but also filled with potential. By proactively addressing ethical and regulatory challenges, we can guide the development of AI and IA in ways that enhance healthcare, respect human values, and contribute to a healthier world. As we continue this journey, let's remember the words of poet and civil rights activist Maya Angelou: "Do the best you can until you know better. Then when you know better, do better." In the ever-evolving landscape of AI and IA in healthcare, this commitment to learning, improvement, and ethical integrity will be our guiding star.

References

BATES, D. W., SARIA, S., Ohno-Machado, L., Shah, A., & Escobar, G. (2014). Big data in health care: using analytics to identify and manage high-risk and high-cost patients. Health Affairs, 33(7), 1123-1131.

Birnbaum, M. L., Rizvi, A. F., Confino, J., Correll, C. U., & Kane, J. M. (2017). Role of social media and the Internet in pathways to care for adolescents and young adults with psychotic disorders and non-psychotic mood disorders. Early intervention in psychiatry, 11(4), 290-295.

Bodenstedt, S., Wagner, M., Müller-Stich, B., Weitz, J., & Speidel, S. (2020). Artificial Intelligence-Assisted Surgery: Potential and Challenges. Visceral Medicine, 36, 450 - 455. https://doi.org/10.1159/000511351.

Bresnick, J. (2018). Top 12 Ways Artificial Intelligence Will Impact Healthcare. HealthITAnalytics. Retrieved from https://healthitanalytics.com/news/top-12-ways-artificial-intelligence-will-impact-healthcare.

Chen, Y., Argentinis, J. E., & Weber, G. (2016). IBM Watson: how cognitive computing can be applied to big data challenges in life sciences research. *Clinical therapeutics*, 38(4), 688-701.

Esteva, A., Kuprel, B., Novoa, R. A., Ko, J., Swetter, S. M., Blau, H. M., & Thrun, S. (2017). Dermatologist-level classification of skin cancer with deep neural networks. Nature, 542(7639), 115-118.

Firth, J., Torous, J., Nicholas, J., Carney, R., Pratap, A., Rosenbaum, S., & Sarris, J. (2017). The efficacy of smartphone-based mental health interventions for depressive symptoms: a meta-analysis of randomized controlled trials. World psychiatry, 16(3), 287-298.

Hollander, J. E., & Carr, B. G. (2020). Virtually perfect? Telemedicine for Covid-19. The New England journal of medicine, 382(18), 1679-1681.

Jiang, F., Jiang, Y., Zhi, H., Dong, Y., Li, H., Ma, S., ... & Wang, Y. (2017). Artificial intelligence in healthcare: past, present and future. Stroke and Vascular Neurology, 2(4), 230-243.

Jiang, F., Jiang, Y., Zhi, H., Dong, Y., Li, H., Ma, S., Wang, Y., Dong, Q., Shen, H., & Wang, Y. (2017). Artificial intelligence in healthcare: past, present and future. Stroke and Vascular Neurology, 2(4), 230–243.

Kohli, M., & Tan, S. S. (2016). Electronic health records: how can IS researchers contribute to transforming healthcare? MIS Quarterly, 40(3), 553-573

Korolev, S., Safiullin, A., Belyaev, M., & Dodonova, Y. (2017, April). Residual and plain convolutional neural networks for 3D brain MRI classification. In *2017 IEEE 14th international symposium on biomedical imaging (ISBI 2017)* (pp. 835-838). IEEE.

Krittanawong, C., Zhang, H., Wang, Z., Aydar, M., & Kitai, T. (2017). Artificial intelligence in precision cardiovascular medicine. *Journal of the American College of Cardiology*, 69(21), 2657-2664.

Krittanawong, C., Zhang, H., Wang, Z., Aydar, M., & Kitai, T. (2017). Artificial intelligence in precision cardiovascular medicine. *Journal of the American College of Cardiology*, 69(21), 2657-2664.

Rajkomar, A., Hardt, M., Howell, M. D., Corrado, G., & Chin, M. H. (2018). Ensuring fairness in machine learning to advance health equity. Annals of internal medicine, 169(12), 866-872.

Rajkomar, A., Oren, E., Chen, K., Dai, A. M., Hajaj, N., Hardt, M., ... & Sundberg, P. (2018). Scalable and accurate deep learning with electronic health records. NPJ Digital Medicine, 1(1), 1-10.

Rumbold, J. M. M., & Pierscionek, B. K. (2017). The effect of the General Data Protection Regulation on medical research. Journal of medical Internet research, 19(2), e47.

Steinhubl, S. R., Muse, E. D., & Topol, E. J. (2015). The emerging field of mobile health. Science translational medicine, 7(283), 283rv3-283rv3.

Swan, M. (2012). Health 2050: The realization of personalized medicine through crowdsourcing, the Quantified Self, and the participatory biocitizen. Journal of personalized medicine, 2(3), 93-118.

Topol, E. (2019). High-performance medicine: the convergence of human and artificial intelligence. Nature Medicine, 25, 44–56.

Topol, E. J. (2019). High-performance medicine: the convergence of human and artificial intelligence. Nature Medicine, 25(1), 44–56.

Vayena, E., Blasimme, A., & Cohen, I. G. (2018). Machine learning in medicine: Addressing ethical challenges. PLoS Medicine, 15(11), e1002689.

Wiens, J., Saria, S., Sendak, M., Ghassemi, M., Liu, V. X., Doshi-Velez, F., Jung, K., Heller, K., Kale, D., Saeed, M., Ossorio, P. N., Thadaney-Israni, S., & Goldenberg, A. (2019). Do no harm: a roadmap for responsible machine learning for health care. Nature Medicine, 25, 1337–1340.

Chapter 8: The Future of AI and IA

Envisioning the Future of AI and IA

AS WE STAND ON THE precipice of an era marked by rapid technological advancements, the realms of Artificial Intelligence (AI) and Intelligence Augmentation (IA) beckon us to ponder their future landscapes. Given their profound influence on nearly every aspect of life, including healthcare, business, education, and transportation, we must consider their paths ahead.

The future of AI and IA is not a predetermined destination but a journey shaped by human ambition, innovation, and our collective vision for a society interwoven with technology (Bostrom, 2014).

The Continual Evolution of AI and IA

A FUNDAMENTAL CHARACTERISTIC of both AI and IA is their continual evolution. As these technologies advance, we continually redefine their boundaries, potential applications, and impact on our world. This evolution is driven by technological progress and our changing understanding of intelligence, cognition, and what it means to be human in a digitally interconnected world.

AI's pursuit of machines with human-like cognitive abilities continues to inch closer to its objective. At the same time, IA continues to innovate in leveraging technology for extending and enhancing human intellect and capabilities (Kurzweil, 2005).

The story of AI and IA is, at its core, a human story. It's a narrative about our desires to transcend limitations, solve complex problems, and enhance our collective human experience. It is, therefore, a story that will continue to evolve as long as we, as a society, continue to imagine, invent, and innovate.

Projecting Trends and Advancements

WHILE AN UNCERTAIN endeavor, projecting the trends and advancements in AI and IA is an essential exercise to anticipate their potential implications. Current developments suggest exciting trajectories for both.

AI is increasingly moving toward more autonomous systems capable of learning and adapting in complex environments, with advancements in deep learning and neural networks leading the way (LeCun, Bengio & Hinton, 2015). Simultaneously, the fusion of AI and IA is becoming more seamless, with IA systems utilizing AI capabilities to augment human intelligence better.

The potential applications of AI and IA are virtually limitless, from smart homes that anticipate our needs to augmented reality systems that enhance our interactions with the world to AI systems that assist doctors in diagnosing diseases. These technologies promise not only to transform the way we live, work, and play but also to redefine our understanding of intelligence and human potential.

Future Trends in AI

THE FUTURE OF ARTIFICIAL Intelligence (AI) paints a fascinating picture, with its narratives intertwined with our personal and professional lives. As we advance further into the 21st century, AI is anticipated to reshape the landscape of our society in significant ways. Its applications and influences are predicted to penetrate deeper into realms we're just beginning to explore. While this progression brings immense potential, it's not without challenges and ethical dilemmas.

Progress toward General AI

GENERAL AI, OR ARTIFICIAL General Intelligence (AGI), has long been the holy grail of AI research. It refers to machines that possess the ability to understand, learn, and apply knowledge across a wide range of tasks at a level equivalent to, or even exceeding, human intelligence (Goertzel & Pennachin, 2007). While current AI applications are largely centered around Narrow AI, which is designed for specific tasks, significant strides are being made toward the development of AGI.

Although we are still in the nascent stages of achieving this feat, the impact of AGI would be transformational. From comprehensively assisting in scientific research to potentially addressing complex societal challenges, the promise of AGI could revolutionize our approach to problem-solving.

The Increasing Role of AI in Decision-Making

AI'S ROLE IN DECISION-making processes is expected to expand significantly. Leveraging its ability to process vast amounts of data and uncover patterns beyond human capabilities, AI is set to transform decision-making in various fields. This includes critical areas such as healthcare, where AI could assist in diagnostics and treatment planning, and the public sector, where it could help with policy decisions (Raghupathi & Raghupathi, 2014). Integrating AI in decision-making can drastically enhance operations' efficiency, accuracy, and scalability.

However, as AI plays a more prominent role in decision-making, the need for transparency and interpretability becomes paramount. The rise of Explainable AI (XAI) reflects this trend, aiming to make AI decision-making processes more understandable and trustworthy for humans (Gunning et al., 2019).

AI and Privacy: New Approaches for Data Handling

AI'S INCREASING DATA handling and processing capabilities have resulted in enhanced personalized services, improved business operations, and innovative solutions to complex problems. However, it also raises significant privacy concerns. As we move forward, new approaches are anticipated to balance the use of data-driven AI applications and individuals' privacy rights. One such approach is the concept of privacy-preserving machine learning, which involves training AI models without accessing raw data, thus preserving privacy. Technologies like differential privacy and federated learning are promising developments in this direction (Abadi et al., 2016; Konečný et al., 2016).

In the future, AI will likely continue to weave itself into the fabric of our society, reshaping it in ways we are only beginning to imagine. However, as we embrace this AI-infused future, it is vital to navigate the journey responsibly, addressing challenges that arise and ensuring the technology is used to benefit all of humanity.

Future Trends in IA

AS WE SHIFT OUR GAZE toward the Intelligence Augmentation (IA) horizon, the landscape teems with exciting possibilities. With its human-centric approach, IA is poised to reshape our relationship with technology and redefine our potential. Below, we explore some of the anticipated trends and advancements in IA.

Advancements in Human-Computer Interaction

ADVANCEMENTS IN HUMAN-computer interaction are a key component of the future of IA. The goal is to develop intuitive, natural ways for humans to interact with technology that goes beyond the traditional mouse-and-keyboard paradigm. Areas like natural language processing, gesture recognition, and brain-computer interfaces are predicted to mature significantly, making our interactions with technology more seamless and intuitive (Preece, Rogers, & Sharp, 2015).

With these advancements, technology could become a more integral part of our daily lives, extending our cognitive capabilities in a discreet, user-friendly manner.

The Rise of Cognitive Augmentation

COGNITIVE AUGMENTATION, a core principle of IA, is set to become increasingly sophisticated. Future IA technologies may not only assist with information processing and decision-making but also augment other cognitive abilities like creativity, problem-solving, and learning. Emerging fields like neurotechnology and cognitive computing hold promising potential. For example, neurofeedback devices could enhance our ability to manage our attention and emotional states, while sophisticated AI algorithms could offer personalized strategies for learning and problem-solving (Kurzweil, 2014).

Personalization and Individual-Centric Approaches in IA

AS IA TECHNOLOGY EVOLVES, it's likely to become more personalized and individual-centric. This means that IA tools will better understand and adapt to individual users' needs, preferences, strengths, and weaknesses.

Advancements in areas such as machine learning and user modeling will drive this trend, enabling IA systems to learn from user interactions and customize their functionality accordingly. This could lead to a more personalized, effective augmentation of individual cognitive abilities (Markoff, 2015).

As we contemplate the future of IA, we should remember the human element at its core. Amid all the technological advancements, the goal of IA remains to enhance human potential, not to replace it.

The Confluence of AI and IA in the Future

AS WE JOURNEY FURTHER into the age of information and computation, the future of both Artificial Intelligence (AI) and Intelligence Augmentation (IA) is expected to intertwine even more profoundly. Thus, there is a pressing need to explore how these two revolutionary fields might collaborate, adapt, and evolve in the coming years, transforming our society and the human experience.

Synergistic Advancements: Where AI and IA Meet

IN THE FUTURE, ADVANCEMENTS in AI and IA are projected to be increasingly symbiotic. Rather than seeing these two fields as competitive, we are starting to recognize the immense potential that lies at their intersection. The future of AI is likely to be more human-centric, embodying the principles of IA. At the same time, IA is expected to harness more sophisticated AI algorithms to amplify human intellect effectively (Davenport & Kirby, 2016).

Predictions for Combined Applications of AI and IA

THE SYNERGISTIC APPROACH toward AI and IA is expected to drive innovative applications that harness both strengths. These applications might include advanced decision-support systems that leverage AI's computational prowess while incorporating human insight, expertise, and judgment.

We might also see advancements in personalized learning and adaptive user interfaces, where AI-powered systems augment human cognition in a tailored, user-specific manner (Bostrom & Yudkowsky, 2014).

Impacts on Society and the Human Experience

AS AI AND IA CONTINUE to converge, they will profoundly shape our society and the human experience. We might see a world where technology serves as a natural extension of our cognition, enhancing our capabilities while respecting our autonomy. Ethical considerations will play an integral role in this future, guiding the development of AI and IA in a manner that prioritizes human well-being, fairness, and inclusivity (Bostrom & Yudkowsky, 2014).

In this exciting era of AI and IA, we are not just observers but active participants. The future isn't simply something that happens to us—it's something we can shape. As we engage with AI and IA, we have the opportunity to guide their evolution, ensuring they reflect our values and serve our collective needs.

Challenges and Opportunities Ahead

AS WE STAND ON THE brink of a future influenced by AI and IA, it is important to be cognizant of the challenges and opportunities that lie ahead.

Addressing Ethical and Social Implications

ONE OF THE GREATEST challenges in the future of AI and IA is the ethical and social implications these technologies engender. Privacy issues, data security, algorithmic bias, and the potential for societal disruption are among the concerns that must be carefully considered. Furthermore, we must ensure that the benefits of AI and IA are equitably distributed, avoiding the creation or exacerbation of social inequalities. Ethical guidelines, policies, public dialogue, and education will be key in navigating these challenges (Crawford & Calo, 2016).

Overcoming Technical and Design Hurdles

IN THE TECHNICAL REALM, creating AI systems that are not just powerful but also transparent, reliable, and user-friendly is a significant challenge. Developing intuitive interfaces and systems that can effectively integrate with human cognition is an ongoing design challenge for IA. Overcoming these hurdles requires cross-disciplinary collaboration, drawing on expertise in areas such as computer science, cognitive psychology, and user experience design (Dove, Halskov, Forlizzi, & Zimmerman, 2017).

Exploiting Opportunities for Innovation and Growth

DESPITE THE CHALLENGES, the future of AI and IA is ripe with opportunities for innovation and growth. These technologies can potentially revolutionize various sectors, from healthcare and education to business and entertainment. For instance, AI can lead to more accurate medical diagnoses, personalized learning experiences, and efficient business operations.

IA can enhance human decision-making, facilitate knowledge creation, and transform our interactions with the digital world. We can harness these opportunities to create a future where technology amplifies our human potential (Bostrom & Yudkowsky, 2014).

Role of Policy, Regulation, and Public Perception

AS AI AND IA CONTINUE to penetrate various aspects of our lives, the roles of policy, regulation, and public perception are becoming increasingly important.

Evolving Regulatory Landscape for AI and IA

AI AND IA TECHNOLOGIES' rapid growth and potential implications have necessitated a new regulatory paradigm. Governments and international organizations are grappling with how to create rules and standards that ensure safety and protect individual rights while fostering innovation.

This includes addressing complex issues around data privacy, AI transparency, and accountability. The challenge lies in maintaining a delicate balance—too heavy-handed regulation could stifle innovation, while a laissez-faire approach could risk unintended negative consequences (Calo & Citron, 2020).

The Influence of Public Perception and Social Acceptance

PUBLIC PERCEPTION PLAYS a pivotal role in the adoption and impact of AI and IA technologies. Misunderstandings and fears around AI could hinder its acceptance, while overhyped expectations could lead to disillusionment. Therefore, educating the public about the realities of these technologies is a key task.

Furthermore, involving diverse societal stakeholders in discussions and decision-making around AI and IA can help ensure that these technologies are developed and used in ways that align with societal values and needs (Cave et al., 2018).

The Importance of Interdisciplinary Dialogue and Collaboration

FINALLY, ADDRESSING the challenges and opportunities of AI and IA requires a truly interdisciplinary approach. This involves collaboration between computer scientists, ethicists, psychologists, policy-makers, and many others. By combining diverse perspectives, we can better understand the broad implications of these technologies and develop thoughtful, inclusive solutions.

Initiatives that promote such interdisciplinary dialogue, from academic conferences to public forums, are therefore crucial as we navigate the future of AI and IA (Vinuesa et al., 2020).

Conclusion: Embracing the AI-IA Synergy

AS WE LOOK TOWARD THE future of AI and IA, we stand on the brink of a new era. An era where technology and humanity intertwine in unprecedented ways.

Reflecting on the Journey Ahead

THE JOURNEY AHEAD PROMISES to be filled with challenges and opportunities alike. As AI continues pushing the boundaries of what machines can do and IA seeks to elevate the human intellect, we are entering a great technological transition. It is a journey that will not only reshape our relationship with technology but also redefine our understanding of intelligence itself. It will involve ethical quandaries, policy debates, and rapid innovation.

Throughout this journey, keeping the human element at the forefront will be essential, ensuring that these technologies enhance our lives rather than complicate them (Russell, 2019).

Final Thoughts on the Transformative Potential of AI and IA

THE CONVERGENCE OF AI and IA has transformative potential. By blending the strengths of machine intelligence and human intellect, the AI-IA synergy could help us tackle complex challenges, streamline decision-making, and usher in new levels of productivity and creativity. However, we must navigate this path cautiously, ensuring we address ethical and societal implications proactively.

As we step into this exciting future, we must remember that these technologies are tools designed by us and for us. The end goal of both AI and IA should always be to enhance our lives and society (Dignum, 2019).

References

ABADI, M., CHU, A., Goodfellow, I., McMahan, H. B., Mironov, I., Talwar, K., & Zhang, L. (2016, October). Deep learning with differential privacy. In *Proceedings of the 2016 ACM SIGSAC conference on computer and communications security* (pp. 308-318).

Bostrom, N. (2014). Superintelligence: Paths, Dangers, Strategies. Oxford: Oxford University Press.

Bostrom, N., & Yudkowsky, E. (2014). The Ethics of Artificial Intelligence. In K. Frankish & W. M. Ramsey (Eds.), The Cambridge Handbook of Artificial Intelligence (pp. 316-334). Cambridge University Press.

Calo, R., & Citron, D. K. (2020). The Automated Administrative State: A Crisis of Legitimacy. Emory Law Journal, 70, 575-596.

Cave, S., Craig, C., Dihal, K., Dillon, S., Montgomery, J., Singler, B., & Taylor, L. (2018). Portrayals and perceptions of AI and why they matter.

Crawford, K., & Calo, R. (2016). There is a blind spot in AI research. Nature, 538(7625), 311-313.

Davenport, T. H., & Kirby, J. (2016). Just How Smart Are Smart Machines? MIT Sloan Management Review, 57(3), 21.

Dignum, V. (2019). *Responsible artificial intelligence: how to develop and use AI in a responsible way* (Vol. 2156). Cham: Springer.

Dove, G., Halskov, K., Forlizzi, J., & Zimmerman, J. (2017, May). UX design innovation: Challenges for working with machine learning as a design material. In *Proceedings of the 2017 chi conference on human factors in computing systems* (pp. 278-288).

Goertzel, B., & Pennachin, C. (Eds.). (2007). Artificial general intelligence (Vol. 2). Springer.

Gunning, D., Stefik, M., Choi, J., Miller, T., Stumpf, S., & Yang, G. Z. (2019). XAI—Explainable artificial intelligence. *Science robotics*, *4*(37), eaay7120.

Konečný, J., McMahan, H. B., Yu, F. X., Richtárik, P., Suresh, A. T., & Bacon, D. (2016). Federated learning: Strategies for improving communication efficiency. *arXiv preprint arXiv:1610.05492.*

Kurzweil, R. (2005). The Singularity is Near: When Humans Transcend Biology. New York: Viking.

Kurzweil, R. (2014). How to Create a Mind: The Secret of Human Thought Revealed. United Kingdom: Duckworth Books.

LeCun, Y., Bengio, Y., & Hinton, G. (2015). Deep learning. Nature, 521(7553), 436–444.

Markoff, J. (2016). Machines of Loving Grace: The Quest for Common Ground Between Humans and Robots. United States: HarperCollins.

Preece, J., Rogers, Y., Sharp, H. (2015). Interaction Design: Beyond Human-Computer Interaction. United Kingdom: Wiley.

Raghupathi, W., & Raghupathi, V. (2014). Big data analytics in healthcare: promise and potential. Health information science and systems, 2(1), 3.

Russell, S. (2019). Human Compatible: Artificial Intelligence and the Problem of Control. Viking.

Vinuesa, R., Azizpour, H., Leite, I., Balaam, M., Dignum, V., Domisch, S., Feliú, A., & Wagner, A. (2020). The role of artificial intelligence in achieving the Sustainable Development Goals. Nature Communications, 11(1), 233-245.

Chapter 9: Conclusion

———

IN THIS RAPIDLY ADVANCING era, cutting-edge technologies like AI and IA have revolutionized various industries, influencing our daily lives in ways we could have only imagined a few decades ago. From self-driving cars to personalized recommendations, AI and IA are changing how we interact with technology and transforming the innovation landscape.

Recap of the Basics

Definition of Artificial Intelligence (AI) and Intelligence Augmentation (IA)

WE EMBARKED ON THIS journey of discovery by understanding what AI and IA are and how they differ. Let us recap a bit.

Artificial Intelligence refers to the simulation of human intelligence in machines programmed to think and learn like humans. This encompasses a wide range of techniques and technologies, from rule-based systems to neural networks, designed to perform tasks that typically require human intelligence. AI can include both narrow AI, which is focused on specific tasks like language translation or image recognition, and general AI, which aims to replicate human-like cognitive abilities.

On the other hand, Intelligence Augmentation is the combination of AI and automation technologies that aim to streamline and optimize processes by automating repetitive tasks, decision-making, and problem-solving. IA encompasses robotic process automation (RPA), cognitive automation, and other intelligent tools that augment human capabilities, leading to increased efficiency and accuracy across various domains.

Understanding these concepts is crucial because AI and IA have rapidly infiltrated various sectors, leading to transformative changes in how we work, communicate, and interact with machines.

Importance and Prevalence of AI and IA in Modern Times

THE SIGNIFICANCE OF AI and IA cannot be overstated, as they have become an integral part of modern society. Their impact spans across industries, including healthcare, finance, manufacturing, marketing, and more.

Healthcare

AI AND IA HAVE PAVED the way for more accurate diagnoses, personalized treatments, and enhanced patient care in the healthcare sector. Machine learning algorithms can analyze vast amounts of medical data to identify patterns and detect diseases at an early stage. Furthermore, robotic surgeries have become increasingly prevalent, allowing for more precise procedures and faster recovery times. AI-driven chatbots and virtual health assistants have also improved patient engagement and support.

Finance

AI AND IA HAVE REVOLUTIONIZED customer service, fraud detection, and risk management in the financial industry. Chatbots and virtual assistants now handle routine customer inquiries, enabling human agents to focus on more complex tasks. AI algorithms can analyze financial data in real-time, making data-driven decisions and mitigating risks more efficiently. Additionally, algorithmic trading and robo-advisors have transformed investment strategies, making them more accessible and cost-effective.

Manufacturing

MANUFACTURING HAS EMBRACED automation and AI-powered robotics, increasing productivity and reducing errors. AI-driven predictive maintenance allows manufacturers to detect and address equipment issues before they cause significant downtime. Collaborative robots (cobots) work alongside human workers, optimizing production processes and ensuring a safer work environment.

Marketing

AI AND IA HAVE TRANSFORMED marketing by enabling hyper-personalized campaigns, targeted advertisements, and customer behavior analysis. Through machine learning, businesses can tailor their offerings to individual preferences, enhancing customer experiences and fostering brand loyalty. Intelligent chatbots engage with customers, providing instant support and facilitating sales, improving overall customer satisfaction.

Social Impact

BEYOND SPECIFIC INDUSTRIES, AI and IA also play a crucial role in addressing societal challenges. For example, AI has been used to predict natural disasters, improve agricultural efficiency, and enhance accessibility for people with disabilities. Furthermore, AI-powered language translation tools break down communication barriers, fostering global collaboration and understanding.

Benefits of AI and IA

AFTER GAINING A BASIC understanding of the concepts, we explored the myriad benefits that Artificial Intelligence (AI) and Intelligence Augmentation (IA) bring to our lives. These revolutionary technologies have already significantly impacted various industries, demonstrating their potential to transform how we work, interact, and thrive.

Automation of Repetitive Tasks

ONE OF AI AND IA'S most immediate and tangible advantages is the automation of repetitive tasks. Mundane and time-consuming activities, which were once a burden on human workers, are now being efficiently handled by intelligent machines. This not only saves time but also enhances human productivity and creativity. By delegating mundane tasks to AI-driven systems, employees can focus on higher-value activities that require critical thinking, problem-solving, and human ingenuity.

Imagine a marketing team that no longer needs to manually send out routine emails or analyze vast amounts of customer data for segmentation. AI-powered marketing automation platforms can handle these tasks effortlessly, allowing marketers to channel their energy into crafting compelling campaigns and devising innovative strategies.

Increased Efficiency and Cost Reduction

THE IMPACT OF AI AND IA on industries like manufacturing and logistics cannot be overstated. Automation in these sectors has streamlined operations, reduced errors, and significantly increased efficiency. In manufacturing, robots and cobots collaborate seamlessly to optimize production processes, resulting in higher output rates and decreased production costs.

Moreover, AI-powered predictive maintenance systems have proven invaluable in preventing costly downtime. These systems analyze data from sensors and machinery to predict potential failures, enabling proactive maintenance and preventing breakdowns before they occur. This not only saves money but also improves overall equipment reliability.

In logistics, AI-driven route optimization algorithms have revolutionized supply chain management. Businesses can significantly reduce transportation costs and environmental impact by calculating the most efficient delivery routes and optimizing load distribution. This efficiency benefits both the company's bottom line and the planet.

Improved Decision-Making

DATA IS THE LIFEBLOOD of AI and IA, and their potential to leverage large datasets for informed decision-making is one of their most significant advantages. AI algorithms can process and analyze vast amounts of data at incredible speeds, providing insights that humans might miss or take much longer to identify.

AI is becoming an invaluable decision-making tool in industries like finance and healthcare. In finance, sophisticated AI-driven trading algorithms can analyze market trends, identify patterns, and execute trades with incredible accuracy and speed. Similarly, in healthcare, AI-powered systems can process patient data, medical records, and scientific literature to assist doctors in diagnosing complex diseases and recommending personalized treatment plans.

However, it's essential to ensure that the data used by AI systems are diverse, representative, and unbiased to avoid perpetuating existing biases or making flawed decisions based on incomplete information.

Enhanced Customer Experiences

AI AND IA HAVE BROUGHT about a new era of personalized customer experiences. Businesses can gain profound insights into individual preferences, behaviors, and needs by analyzing vast amounts of customer data. This enables them to tailor their products and services to match each customer's unique requirements, fostering a stronger emotional connection with the brand.

E-commerce platforms, for example, leverage AI-driven recommendation engines to suggest products based on a user's browsing history, purchase behavior, and preferences. These personalized recommendations improve the user experience and increase the likelihood of making a purchase.

AI-driven chatbots and virtual assistants have also revolutionized customer service. Customers can now get instant responses to their inquiries, even outside of regular business hours. Armed with natural language processing capabilities, these bots can understand and respond to customer queries effectively, enhancing overall customer satisfaction and loyalty.

Better Risk Management

IDENTIFYING AND MITIGATING risks is crucial for businesses in today's complex and ever-evolving world. AI and IA have stepped in to bolster risk management practices across various industries. In finance, AI algorithms analyze vast datasets to detect fraudulent activities in real-time, preventing potential financial losses for both individuals and institutions.

Moreover, AI-driven security systems help safeguard critical infrastructure, corporate data, and personal information from cyberattacks. These systems can quickly identify suspicious patterns and respond proactively to potential threats, significantly reducing the risk of security breaches.

In the healthcare industry, AI-powered risk prediction models help healthcare providers accurately assess patients' risk profiles. By analyzing patient data and historical trends, these models can identify individuals at high risk of developing certain conditions, enabling timely interventions and preventive measures.

Challenges of AI and IA

THE JOURNEY INTO THE world of AI and IA didn't end there! As we continued our exploration of the fascinating world of Artificial Intelligence (AI) and Intelligence Augmentation (IA), we delved into some of the most pressing challenges that arise with the proliferation of AI and IA technologies.

Job Displacement

ONE OF THE MOST PROMINENT concerns surrounding AI and IA is the potential for job displacement. As automation takes over repetitive and routine tasks, there are valid worries about the workforce, especially for low-skilled workers whose jobs may be at risk. The fear of machines replacing human labor has historical roots, and it resurfaces whenever a new wave of automation emerges.

While AI and IA undoubtedly increase efficiency and productivity, the impact on the job market is not uniform across all industries and occupations. Some jobs may be automated, leading to workforce restructuring, but new roles and opportunities also emerge to complement AI technologies. However, there is a need for upskilling and reskilling the workforce to prepare them for jobs that require a blend of human and AI expertise.

Bias and Discrimination

AI AND IA SYSTEMS ARE only as good as the data they are trained on. The algorithms can perpetuate existing biases and discriminatory practices if the training data is biased or limited. For instance, biased algorithms could unfairly favor certain demographics in hiring or loan approval processes, leading to discrimination and social inequality.

Careful algorithm design and testing are essential to identifying and rectifying biases in AI systems. Moreover, there must be transparency in how AI decisions are made, enabling thorough scrutiny and accountability. As developers and users of AI and IA, it is our responsibility to strive for fairness and inclusivity, ensuring that these technologies work for the betterment of society as a whole.

Security and Privacy Concerns

AI AND IA TECHNOLOGIES heavily rely on data to learn and make informed decisions. While access to large amounts of data enables powerful AI capabilities, it raises concerns about data security and privacy. Gathering, storing, and handling massive volumes of sensitive data requires robust cybersecurity measures to prevent unauthorized access and data breaches.

Additionally, there are concerns about the potential misuse of data for malicious purposes. As AI systems become more sophisticated, so do the methods of exploiting them. Ensuring the safety and privacy of data is crucial not only for individuals but also for organizations and governments that rely on AI and IA technologies.

Complexity

DEVELOPING AND IMPLEMENTING AI and IA solutions require specialized expertise and substantial resources. The complexity of these technologies can be daunting for smaller companies and organizations, limiting their ability to leverage AI to the fullest. As a result, there is a risk of widening the technological gap between large corporations and smaller enterprises.

To address this challenge, collaborations between industry leaders and startups and government support for research and development can foster innovation and accessibility. Moreover, there is a need for user-friendly AI tools and platforms that empower a broader range of users to leverage AI and IA technologies effectively.

Ethical Concerns

ETHICAL CONSIDERATIONS become paramount as AI and IA technologies become more deeply integrated into our lives. From autonomous vehicles making life-and-death decisions to AI-powered healthcare systems determining treatment plans, ethical dilemmas arise in various critical areas.

AI systems should be designed to prioritize human values and well-being. Transparent decision-making processes and mechanisms for human oversight are vital to ensure that AI and IA technologies align with human values and societal norms.

For example, ensuring patient autonomy, privacy, and the ability to override AI recommendations is crucial in the healthcare industry. Ethical considerations extend to areas like AI in criminal justice, where fairness and accountability are paramount, and AI in education, where student data privacy and the impact on pedagogy must be carefully assessed.

Importance of Responsible Development and Integration of AI and IA in Society

AS WE NEARED THE CONCLUSION of our journey through the world of Artificial Intelligence (AI) and Intelligence Augmentation (IA), we came to a critical aspect that demands our utmost attention: the responsible development and integration of these transformative technologies into society. AI and IA have the potential to reshape the world we live in, offering countless benefits and opportunities. However, with great power comes great responsibility, and addressing the challenges and implications they present is vital.

Transformative Impact of AI and IA on Society

THE TRANSFORMATIVE impact of AI and IA on society is undeniable. We experience it in our daily lives, often without even realizing it. AI and IA have become integral to modern living, from virtual assistants that help us navigate our schedules to personalized content recommendations that enrich our entertainment experience.

In healthcare, AI-powered medical imaging systems enable faster and more accurate diagnoses, potentially saving lives. In education, AI-driven adaptive learning platforms cater to individual student needs, enhancing learning. In transportation, self-driving cars promise safer roads and increased mobility for all. These examples merely scratch the surface of the vast array of AI and IA applications.

Recognizing the Need for Responsibility

THE WIDESPREAD INTEGRATION of AI and IA technologies also comes with challenges and potential risks. We must recognize the need for responsibility to ensure that the benefits of these technologies outweigh their drawbacks. Responsible development involves addressing issues such as bias and discrimination in algorithms, privacy concerns in data collection, and potential job displacement.

As AI and IA technologies evolve, there is a responsibility to safeguard against their misuse or unintended consequences. This involves continuously evaluating the impact of these technologies on society and proactively taking steps to mitigate any negative effects.

Collaboration of Stakeholders

ADDRESSING THE CHALLENGES and ensuring responsible integration of AI and IA requires collaboration among various stakeholders. Governments, businesses, communities, and individuals all play pivotal roles in shaping the future of these technologies.

Governments can establish clear guidelines and regulations that promote ethical AI development, protect data privacy, and ensure fairness in AI applications. They can also invest in AI education and training programs to equip the workforce with the skills necessary to thrive in an AI-driven world.

As creators and adopters of AI and IA technologies, businesses must prioritize transparency and accountability in their AI systems. They should invest in robust testing and validation processes to minimize bias and discrimination, ensuring that AI-driven decisions align with human values.

Communities should actively engage in discussions about AI and IA developments that affect them. Public input is essential in defining these technologies' boundaries and acceptable use. Transparent communication and public consultations can foster trust and cooperation between communities and AI developers.

Involvement of the Public

IN THE ERA OF AI AND IA, involving the public in decision-making is crucial. These technologies impact society as a whole, and public input can provide diverse perspectives and valuable insights. Engaging the public in discussions about AI ethics, regulations, and guidelines ensures that AI is used responsibly and aligned with societal values.

Building trust between the public and AI developers is paramount. Open communication and transparency about how AI systems function, what data is collected, and how it is used can allay fears and misconceptions. Additionally, ensuring data privacy and security further reinforces public confidence in AI technologies.

Balancing Benefits and Risks

THE RESPONSIBLE DEVELOPMENT and integration of AI and IA hinge on striking a balance between maximizing their benefits and mitigating potential risks. AI and IA technologies have enormous potential to drive progress, enhance efficiency, and improve the quality of life for individuals and society at large.

To achieve this balance, continuous evaluation and feedback are necessary. Regular assessments of AI systems, their impact, and potential biases can help fine-tune the technologies and ensure their alignment with ethical principles. Responsible AI development requires a dynamic approach that adapts to the changing needs of society.

As we look to the future, there is much reason for hope. By embracing the challenges and responsibly navigating the complexities of AI and IA, we can foster a balanced and positive impact on society. With careful attention to the ethical implications and collaboration among stakeholders, AI and IA can truly become tools that uplift humanity, drive progress, and enhance the quality of life for all.

We stand at the cusp of a new era where human ingenuity and AI-powered technologies can work hand in hand to overcome challenges, address societal needs, and unlock new frontiers of human potential. The journey into the world of AI and IA is a continuous one. Our shared responsibility is to shape its course, ensuring that these transformative technologies remain a force for good in the world.

References

ABADI, M., CHU, A., Goodfellow, I., McMahan, H. B., Mironov, I., Talwar, K., & Zhang, L. (2016, October). Deep learning with differential privacy. In *Proceedings of the 2016 ACM SIGSAC conference on computer and communications security* (pp. 308-318).

Bostrom, N. (2014). Superintelligence: Paths, Dangers, Strategies. Oxford: Oxford University Press.

Bostrom, N., & Yudkowsky, E. (2014). The Ethics of Artificial Intelligence. In K. Frankish & W. M. Ramsey (Eds.), The Cambridge Handbook of Artificial Intelligence (pp. 316-334). Cambridge University Press.

Calo, R., & Citron, D. K. (2020). The Automated Administrative State: A Crisis of Legitimacy. Emory Law Journal, 70, 575-596.

Cave, S., Craig, C., Dihal, K., Dillon, S., Montgomery, J., Singler, B., & Taylor, L. (2018). Portrayals and perceptions of AI and why they matter.

Crawford, K., & Calo, R. (2016). There is a blind spot in AI research. Nature, 538(7625), 311-313.

Davenport, T. H., & Kirby, J. (2016). Just How Smart Are Smart Machines? MIT Sloan Management Review, 57(3), 21.

Dignum, V. (2019). *Responsible artificial intelligence: how to develop and use AI in a responsible way* (Vol. 2156). Cham: Springer.

Dove, G., Halskov, K., Forlizzi, J., & Zimmerman, J. (2017, May). UX design innovation: Challenges for working with machine learning as a design material. In *Proceedings of the 2017 chi conference on human factors in computing systems* (pp. 278-288).

Goertzel, B., & Pennachin, C. (Eds.). (2007). Artificial general intelligence (Vol. 2). Springer.

Gunning, D., Stefik, M., Choi, J., Miller, T., Stumpf, S., & Yang, G. Z. (2019). XAI—Explainable artificial intelligence. *Science robotics*, *4*(37), eaay7120.

Konečný, J., McMahan, H. B., Yu, F. X., Richtárik, P., Suresh, A. T., & Bacon, D. (2016). Federated learning: Strategies for improving communication efficiency. *arXiv preprint arXiv:1610.05492*.

Kurzweil, R. (2005). The Singularity is Near: When Humans Transcend Biology. New York: Viking.

Kurzweil, R. (2014). How to Create a Mind: The Secret of Human Thought Revealed. United Kingdom: Duckworth Books.

LeCun, Y., Bengio, Y., & Hinton, G. (2015). Deep learning. Nature, 521(7553), 436–444.

Markoff, J. (2016). Machines of Loving Grace: The Quest for Common Ground Between Humans and Robots. United States: HarperCollins.

Preece, J., Rogers, Y., Sharp, H. (2015). Interaction Design: Beyond Human-Computer Interaction. United Kingdom: Wiley.

Raghupathi, W., & Raghupathi, V. (2014). Big data analytics in healthcare: promise and potential. Health information science and systems, 2(1), 3.

Russell, S. (2019). Human Compatible: Artificial Intelligence and the Problem of Control. Viking.

Vinuesa, R., Azizpour, H., Leite, I., Balaam, M., Dignum, V., Domisch, S., Feliú, A., & Wagner, A. (2020). The role of artificial intelligence in achieving the Sustainable Development Goals. Nature Communications, 11(1), 233-245.

www.ingramcontent.com/pod-product-compliance
Lightning Source LLC
Chambersburg PA
CBHW061321120726
48001CB00002B/628